STAN JARVIS

Discovering First Names

First Names

SHIRE PUBLICATIONS

Contents

The publishers acknowledge with gratitude the assistance of Rachel Beckett in preparing this book for publication.

British Library Cataloguing in Publication Data: Jarvis, S.M. (Stanley Melville), 1926- Discovering first names. – (Discovering; 289) 1. Names, Personal – Great Britain I. Title 929.4'4'0941 ISBN 0 7478 0383 8.

Printed in Great Britain by CIT Printing Services Ltd, Press Buildings, Merlins Bridge, Haverfordwest, Pembrokeshire SA61 1XF.

Preface

In 1973 I was pondering over the preface to the first edition of
Discovering Christian Names. That book went into three editions
and three reprints. In the intervening years the world has moved on
so fast that a thorough-going revision is again necessary. The op-
portunity has been taken to include half as many names again,
including many, such as Madonna, that would have been unaccept-
able to an earlier generation but have now become commonplace in
a society that names its children from the day they are born without
confirmation by christening.

The completely random way in which we choose forenames today makes rather a mockery of the orderly evolution of the rules by
which man named his progeny through thousands of years.
Onomastics, the study of proper names, cannot account for some of
the stranger appellations dreamed up by fond parents without a
thought of the embarrassment caused to their children in school and
in later life. Onomastics has, however, laid out for us a conspectus
of the naming of individuals. It began in days beyond our imagina-
tion. The Semitic family of names spread out from the cradle of
civilisation in the Middle East. One of the languages it embraced is
Hebrew, and the Bible is a vast storehouse of its names. They
carried an implicit message about their bearers. For instance, Jacob
means 'taking by the heel' – in other words he was born, unusually,
feet first. Ham means 'from the hot lands' – an immigrant from the
south. Kerenhappuch can be interpreted 'pot of eye make-up', implying a surfeit of feminine vanity!

As wave after wave of settlers spread around the globe this system of naming could not cope, and a further division was necessary
to provide individual identity. What was easier than to divide by the
name of the father, in other words patronymics? Peter son of Peter
became Peter Peterson, acquiring a forename and a surname. Simon
bar Jonas meant Simon son of Jonah. So this system of patronymics
was adopted from the Middle East to Scandinavia.

The ancient Greeks had a separate system, using the genitive
form of the father's name to designate the child. That became their
surname, while the father chose his children's forenames and would
alter them if he so wished. Even in those days nicknames were
common. Plato, the great philosopher who lived around 400 BC,
was named Aristocles, but because of his broadness he gained the
equivalent Greek nickname *Platon* and it stuck.

The Roman system was much more complicated. Their highly
ordered society brought into use a triple-name system – the

praenomen or personal name, the *nomen* or family name, and the *cognomen*, which was the equivalent of a nickname. One such name was Caesar, 'the hairy one', which eventually became the accepted family name for the famous family.

The Teutonic races had a simple but effective system in which a combination of two words was chosen from a stock of recognised name-making words. It is from this source that Anglo-Saxon names derived, making up a large part of the British national heritage of names.

In the earliest days a child was given a name at puberty, the time of initiation as an adult. The custom of Christian baptism linked with that pagan initiation but brought forward the time of naming to as soon after the birth as possible, claiming souls for Christ before the devil could influence them. Through the holy scriptures and their vast reservoir of names the stock of baptismal names was much enriched. In modern times the desire to identify an individual very closely in a rapidly increasing population has led to the invention or adaptation of names on which the Victorian parson would have looked with disapproval. The advent of the modern world of entertainment has introduced names that are different from the common herd and are memorable.

'Indian names are most often quite significant. These may be a family's expression of gratitude to a deity for the blessings received or the wishes fulfilled or an association with a person, place, event or time, or even a desire to induce some virtues in the offspring' – Dharma Vira, Governor of West Bengal, 1st March 1969.

According to the national records of births kept at the General Register Office the most popular first names under which babies were registered in 1996 are, in order of popularity:

Girls: 1 Sophie, 2 Chloe, 3 Emily, 4 Megan, 5 Jessica, 6 Lauren, 7 Rebecca, 8 Charlotte, 9 Hannah, 10 Amy.

Boys: 1 Jack, 2 Daniel, 3 Thomas, 4 James, 5 Joshua, 6 Matthew, 7 Ryan, 8 Samuel, 9 Joseph, 10 Liam.

I thank the hundreds of people I have questioned about their first names. With so many people coming from overseas to live in Britain these days we are introduced to many new names from other cultures and languages. Those shown as '(Hindu)' were introduced by the Aryans of North India. Names from Hindustani and Arabic echo the languages of waves of new settlers in Hindustan. Names from Sanskrit, Hindi, Persian and Turkish are also included.

Meanings of names

AAKESH—**m** 'Lord of the sky' (Hindu).

AAKIL—**m** 'Intelligent' (Hindu).

AAMIN—**m** 'Grace of God' (Hindu).

AARON—**m** 'Light' (Hebrew). First high priest of the Israelites.

ABBA—**m** 'Father' (Hindu). Made fashionable as the name of the pop group 'Abba' – with hits in the 1970s; disbanded in 1982.

ABBIE—**f** Short form of Abigail.

ABDIEL—**m** 'Servant of God' (Hebrew).

ABDULLA—**m** 'Servant of God' (Arabic – properly Abd-Allah). One of the most common names in the Arab world, borne by a number of Islamic leaders. Abdullah, King of Jordan, was assassinated in 1951.

ABEL—**m** 'Son' (Hebrew). Second son of Adam, slain by his brother Cain. Abel Magwitch, character in Dickens's *Great Expectations*.

ABIAH—**m** 'My father is the Lord' (Hebrew).

ABIEL—**m** Alternative of Abiah.

ABIGAIL—**f** 'Father's joy' (Hebrew). Wife of David, king of Israel.

ABILENE—**f** Region of the Holy Land and several places in USA, including town where President Dwight D. Eisenhower grew up.

ABIUD—**m** 'Father in glory' (Hebrew).

ABNER—**m** 'Father of light' (Hebrew). Commander of Saul's army, but more recently popularised by the American 'Li'l Abner' strip cartoon.

ABOULHAKIM—**m** 'He who serves Allah' (Hindu).

ABRA—**f** 'Mother of multitudes' (Hebrew).

ABRAHAM—**m** 'Father of a multitude' (Hebrew). Traditional progenitor of the Hebrew people. Abraham Lincoln (1809-65) – sixteenth President of the USA.

ABRAM—**m** Variant of Abraham with the distinct meaning 'high father'.

ABSALOM—**m** 'Peace of the father' (Hebrew). Third son of David, king of Israel. The young clerk in Chaucer's 'Miller's Tale'.

ACHILLES—**m** Its original Greek meaning is obscure. Great warrior of the Trojan Wars as told in Greek legend.

ACIMA—**f** 'The Lord will judge' (Hebrew).

ADA—**f** Probably shortened form of Adela. Byron's daughter (born 1815).

ADAH—**f** 'An ornament' (Hebrew). One of the wives of Esau. The wife of Cain. Adah Mencken, late nineteenth-century American actress and poet.

ADAIR—**m** 'Ford by the oak' (Celtic).

ADALGISA—**f** 'Noble hostage' (Italian, Teutonic origin). Died out in the middle ages but revived since the nineteenth century through the character in Bellini's opera *Norma* (1831).

ADALHARD, ADLARD—**m** 'Noble and strong' (Teutonic).

ADAM—**m** 'Red earth' (Hebrew). The first man, as written in the book of Genesis. Adam Smith wrote *The Wealth of Nations* (1776). *Adam Bede* by George Eliot (1859).

ADAR—**f** 'Fire' (Hebrew). The sixth month of the Jewish Year.

ADELA—**f** 'Noble' (Teutonic). Fourth daughter of William the Conqueror, mother of King Stephen.

ADELAIDE—**f** 'Nobility' (Teutonic). The popular queen (1792-1849) of William IV (reigned 1830-7) made it fashionable. Capital of South Australia, founded 1836, named after her.

ADÈLE—**f** French form of Adela.

ADELGAR—**m** 'Noble spear' (Teutonic).

ADELHEID—**f** German form of Adelaide.

ADELINA, ADELINE—**f** Diminutive of Adela even from Norman times. Adelina Patti (1843-1919), great soprano. 'Sweet Adeline', song popular before First World War.

ADELPHO—**m** 'Brother' (Greek).

ADIBA—**f** 'Cultured' (Arabic).

ADINA—**f** 'Desire' (Hebrew). Shown as a male name in the Old Testament, but now used for girls. 'Adine' – character in Donizetti's opera *L'Elisir d'Amore*.

ADLAI—**m** 'God is just' (Hebrew). Father of one of King David's herdsmen. Adlai Stevenson (1900-65), American politician.

ADOLF, ADOLPH—**m** 'Noble wolf' (Teutonic). Also as Adolphus. Less popular since it was Hitler's forename.

ADONCIA—**f** 'Sweet' (Spanish).

ADONIA—**f** (Greek). 'Beautiful goddess of the resurrection' – signifying the eternal renewal of youth.

ADRIA—**f** A modern feminine form of Adrian.

ADRIAN—**m** 'Of the Adriatic' (Latin). From Hadrian (76-138), the Roman emperor responsible for Hadrian's Wall. Pope Adrian IV, the name adopted by Nicholas Brakespeare (1100-59), the only Englishman to become pope.

ADRIANA—**f** Form of Adrian. A character in Shakespeare's *Comedy of Errors*.

ADRIEL—**m** 'From God's congregation' (Hebrew).

ADRIENNE—**f** French, and more popular, form of Adriana.

AEGIDIUS—**m** The original Latin name translated as Giles.

AENEAS—**m** (Old Irish). The name of the son of Anchises and Aphrodite in classical legend, possibly from greek *ainein,* 'to praise'. It was later used by Irish and Scots as a rendering of the root of Angus.

AERONA—**f** 'Berry' (Welsh). The name may also have a link with the Celtic goddess of battle, Agrona.

AFDAL—**m** 'Excellent' (Arabic).

AFFRICA—**f** 1990s adaptation of the name of the continent.

AGAFYA—**f** (Russian). Derived from the Greek word for 'love'.

AGATHA—**f** 'Good woman' (Greek). St Agatha was a third-century martyr.

AGLAIA—**f** 'Beauty' (Greek). One of the three Graces in Greek mythology.

AGNES—**f** 'Pure' (Greek). St Agnes was a child martyr in the third century. 'From the twelfth to the sixteenth century Agnes was one of the commonest English f. names' (Withycombe). Victorian popularity helped by Keats's 'Eve of St Agnes' (1819) and Tennyson's 'St Agnes Eve' (1842).

AGOSTINO—**m** Italian form of Augustine.

AGUSTIN—**m** Spanish form of Augustine.

AHMED—**m** 'Most highly praised' (Arabic).

AHSAN—**m** 'Gratitude' (Hindu).

AHUVA—**f** Modern name from Hebrew for 'beloved'.

AIDAN—**m** 'Little fire' (Old Irish). Irish monk (died 651), founder of the church in Northumbria.

AILEEN—**f** Form of Eileen more common in Ireland.

AILIS—**f** Irish Gaelic form of Alice.

AILSA—**f** Modern name from nostalgia for Ailsa Craig, islet in the Clyde estuary.

AIMÉE—**f** 'Beloved' (French). Now used in English without the accent.

AINE—**f** Form of Aidan which is also spelt Aithne. In French, *aîné(e)* means eldest child.

AINSLEY—**m** (occasionally **f**). Surname of powerful family in the Scottish borders.

AISHA—**f** 'Alive and well' (Hindu from Arabic). Mohammed's favourite wife.

AJAX—**m** (Greek). A suitor of Helen of Troy and protagonist in the Trojan War. The name may mean an eagle or it may relate to

Job ('weeper').

AKBAR—**m** 'Great' (Arabic). Derived from Akbar the Great (1542-1605), a Muslim king.

AKILINA—**f** 'Eagle'. Russian form of Aquila, hence St Aquilina, virgin martyr of the third century.

ALAN—**m** A Celtic name of uncertain meaning, introduced to England by Alan, Earl of Brittany, at the Conquest.

ALANA—**f** 'My child' (Irish).

ALANDA—**f** A recent amalgamation of Alan and Amanda.

ALARD—**m** Contracton of Adalhard.

ALARIC—**m** 'Ruler over all' (Teutonic). King of the Visigoths (370-410), conqueror of Rome.

ALASTAIR—**m** Scottish form of Alexander.

ALASTOR—**m** 'Avenger' (Greek).

ALAYNA—**f** Feminine form of Alan only recently invented.

ALBAN—**m** 'Of Alba' (Latin). Alba was the name given to towns on a 'white' hill. St Alban, first British martyr (c.300), gave his name to St Albans.

ALBANY—**m** or **f** Derived from towns and districts in USA, Australia and Scotland.

ALBERGA—**m** 'Noble protector' (Teutonic).

ALBERIC—**m** 'Wise ruler' (Teutonic). Reintroduced by Normans in the form of Aubrey.

ALBERT—**m** From Adalbert, 'Nobly bright' (Teutonic). Prince Albert (1819-61) married Queen Victoria in 1840.

ALBERTA—**f** Form of the popular Victorian male name, but also relates to the Canadian province.

ALBERTINE—**f** French diminutive of Alberta. Character in Proust's *Remembrance of Things Past* (1932).

ALBINA—**f** Form of Albinus. St Albina martyred at Caesarea in 250.

ALBINUS—**m** 'White' (Latin). English prelate and scholar (c.737-804), usually known as Alcuin.

ALBREDA—**m** 'Elf counsel' (Teutonic), interpreted as 'wise counsel'.

ALCINA—**f** 'Maid from the sea' (Greek).

ALCUIN—**m** See under Albinus.

ALDA—**f** 'Old' (Teutonic). Sister of Oliver and wife of Orlando in the Charlemagne romances.

ALDEN—**m** 'Old friend' (Old English).

ALDHELM—**m** 'Great helmet' (Old English). Probably signifying warrior. St Aldhelm, abbot of Malmesbury (c.640-709). St Aldhelm's Head on the Dorset coast is corrupted to St Alban's Head.

ALDITH—**f** 'Great in war' (Teutonic).

ALDO—**m** 'Old' (Teutonic). Name in its own right but also

diminutive of Aldous.

ALDOUS—**m** A variant of names beginning with the element Ald- (Teutonic). Aldous Huxley (1894–1963), author of *Brave New World* (1932) and many other important works.

ALDRED—**m** 'Great counsel' (Old English). The Archbishop of York who crowned William the Conqueror in 1066.

ALDWIN—**m** 'Great friend' (Old English). Gave rise to surnames Aldin, Alden, etc.

ALEC—**m** Short form of Alexander.

ALEIDA—**f** Form of Adelheid, thus Adelaide.

ALEM—**m** 'Wise man' (Arabic).

ALENA—**f** Affectionate shortening of Magdalena.

ALETHEA, ALETHIA—**f** 'Truth' (Greek). Alethea Bigge was Jane Austen's friend. Charles I, when Prince of Wales, went to Spain to make the acquaintance of Princess Maria Aletea. In Ireland, Letty is a diminutive of this name.

ALEX—**m** Short form of Alexander.

ALEXA—**f** Affectionate shortening of Alexandra or Alexis, now used independently.

ALEXANDER—**m** 'Helper of men' (Greek). Alexander the Great (356-323 BC), conqueror of the civilised world. Eight popes have chosen this name.

ALEXANDRA—**f** Form of Alexander. Edward VII's queen (1844-1925).

ALEXENA—**f** Diminutive of Alexandra, or form of Alexis – used at a baptism in 1903.

ALEXIS—**m** or **f** 'Helper' (Greek). Greek dramatist of fourth century BC. Alexis Paul (1847-1901), French playwright and novelist, lifelong friend of Emile Zola. Much used as a male name in Russia, but in the twentieth century popular for girls.

ALFA—**m** or **f** Modern variant of Alpha.

ALFONSO—**m** 'Noble and ready' (Spanish, of Visigothic origin). The name of many kings of Spain.

ALFRED—**m** 'Elf counsel' (Old English), interpreted as 'wise counsel'. Alfred the Great (849-99), king of England. Alfred, Lord Tennyson (1809-92), Poet Laureate.

ALFREDA—**f** Form of Alfred.

ALGAR—**m** 'Elf spear' or 'Noble spear' (Old English). Gives rise to surnames like that of Sir Edward Elgar (1857-1934), English composer.

ALGERNON—**m** 'The whiskered one' (Norman French). The nickname of William de Percy, founder of the great Percy family, later earls and dukes of Northumberland, at the time of William the Conqueror, when most courtiers were clean-shaven.

ALI—**m** 'Greatest' (Arabic).

ALICE—**f** Old French variant of Adelheid. Probably influenced in its nineteenth-century revival by Lewis Carroll's *Alice's Adventures in Wonderland* (1865), named after one of his young friends, Alice Liddell.

ALICIA—**f** Derived from the Latin form of Alice.

ALICK—**m** Form of Alec.

ALINE—**f** A contraction of Adeline.

ALISHA—**f** 'Under God's protection' (Hindu).

ALISON—**f** Scottish diminutive of Alice already popular by the fourteenth century.

ALISSA—**f** Variant of Alice.

ALISTAIR—**m** Form of Alastair.

ALIZA, ALIZAH—**f** Modern Hebrew for 'joy'.

ALLAN—**m** Variant of Alan.

ALLEGRA—**f** 'Cheerful' (Latin).

ALLEN—**m** Variant of Alan.

ALMA—**f** 'Kind' (Latin). However it was probably introduced as a result of the celebrated battle of Alma, in the Crimea (1854). Name of the Queen of Body Castle in Spenser's *Faerie Queene*.

ALMERIA—**f** From the province of south-east Spain. The character in Congreve's *The Mourning Bride* who utters the well-known line 'Music hath charms to soothe a savage breast'.

ALMERIC—**m** 'Work-ruler' (Teutonic). Produced Amory and many other surnames.

ALOISIA—**f** Latinised feminine of Aloysius.

ALOYSIUS—**m** Variant of Louis. St Aloysius died 1591 aged twenty-three, and because of the purity of his life was declared patron saint of youth.

ALPHA—**m** or **f** First letter of Greek alphabet. Could denote first child.

ALPHONSE—**m** French form of Alfonso.

ALPHONSO—**m** Alternative spelling of Alfonso.

ALSTON—**m** 'Noble stone' (Old English), though the first element may also come from the words for 'elf' 'old' or 'temple'. Surname derivation.

ALTHEA—**f** 'Wholesome' (Greek). Immortalised in the famous poem 'To Althea from Prison' by Richard Lovelace (1618-58).

ALTHENA—**f** Modern invented name, perhaps from Althea and Ena.

ALUN—**m** Welsh river and district name, but more widely used as a form of Alan.

ALVA, ALVAH—**f** 'Height' (Hebrew). A biblical name mentioned in Genesis 36:40.

ALVAR—**m** 'Wise warrior' (Old English). Spread through Alvar Liddell (1908-81), BBC announcer.

ALVIN—**m** Form of Alwyn.

ALVINA—**f** Form of Alwyn.

ALWYN—**m** 'Noble friend' (Old English).

ALYS—**f** Modern form of Alice.

ALYSSA—**f** Variant of Alice.

AMABEL—**f** 'Lovable' (Old French, from Latin). Sometimes spelt Amiable.

AMADEA—**f** Form of Amadeus.

AMADEUS—**m** 'Loving God' (Latin). Amadeus V (died 1323), Count of Savoy and ancestor of all the kings of Italy. Wolfgang Amadeus Mozart (1755-91).

AMADIS—**m** Form of Amadeus.

AMALIA—**f** Spanish form of Amelia, from *amal*, 'work' (Teutonic). Popular in Germany through Anna Amalia, Duchess of Saxe-Weimar (1739-1807).

AMANDA—**f** 'Lovable' (Latin). Apparently first appears as a character in Colley Cibber's *Love's Last Shift* (1694) and its sequel *The Relapse* by Sir John Vanbrugh.

AMARYLLIS—**f** Name given to a country girl in Greek literature. Developed through Latin poets to use by English poets like Spenser and Milton. Also the name of an exotic flower, similar to a lily.

AMASA—**m** 'Burden bearer' (Hebrew).

AMATO—**m** 'Beloved' (Italian). Two seventh-century saints bear this name.

AMBAR—**m** 'Sky' (Hindi).

AMBER—**f** A modern precious stone name.

AMBROSE—**m** 'Immortal' (Greek). St Ambrose (*c*.339-97), Bishop of Milan in the fourth century, was one of the 'fathers' of the early church.

AMBROSINE—**f** Form of Ambrose. Modern French import.

AMELIA—**f** From *amal*, 'work' (Teutonic), or from the Roman family name Aemilius. In England more often represented by Emily. Princess Amelia, youngest daughter of George III, was called Emily in everyday life. Henry Fielding wrote *Amelia* in 1751. See also Amalia.

AMELIE—**f** Anglicised French form of Amelia, dispensing with accent.

AMERIGO—**m** (Italian). Form of Henry used from the twelfth century. Amerigo Vespucci (1454-1512), explorer, gave his name to America.

AMERY—**m** Form of Amory.

AMIAZ—**m** 'My people are strong' (Jewish). A recent introduction.

AMICE—**f** 'Beloved' (Latin). Very popular in medieval times, but has lost ground to Amy.

AMICIA—**f** 'Beloved' – form of Amice.

AMIJAD—**m** 'Glorious' (Arabic).

AMIN—**m** 'Trustworthy', 'honest' (Arabic).

AMITY—**f** 'Friendship'. A post-Reformation 'abstract quality' name.

AMOLI—**f** 'Precious' (Hindu).

AMORET—**f** Origin uncertain; most likely from the French *amourette*, a 'love affair', but already in use in England in this form in the sixteenth century. Used by Spenser in his *Faerie Queene* (1590). 'Amoret is the type of female loveliness and wifely affection, soft, warm, chaste, gentle and ardent; not sensual nor yet platonic, but that living, breathing, warm-hearted love which fits woman for the fond mother and faithful wife' (Brewer's *Reader's Handbook*).

AMORY—**m** See Almeric.

AMOS—**m** 'Carried' (Hebrew). An Old Testament prophet.

AMPARO—**f** 'Protection' (Spanish). Enshrines the protection offered to Christians through the intervention of the Virgin Mary.

AMRAM—**m** 'Life' (Arabic).

AMUL—**m** 'Priceless treasure' (Hindu).

AMUND—**m** 'Awesome protector' (Old Norse).

AMY—**f** English version of Aimée. Amy Robsart married Robert Dudley, Earl of Leicester, in 1550 but died mysteriously during his suit for the hand of Elizabeth I.

AMYAS—**m** 'Loving God' (Latin). Form of Amadeus. Amyas Leigh, hero of Kingsley's *Westward Ho!* (1855).

ANACLETO—**m** 'He who is called to service' (Greek).

ANAND—**m** 'Delight' (Hindu), from Ananda.

ANANDITA—**f** 'Bringer of joy' (Hindu).

ANANYA—**m** 'Unique' (Hindu).

ANASTASIA—**f** 'She who will rise again' (Greek). Often used for girls born at Easter time. The daughter of the last tsar of Russia, alleged to have survived the assassination of the entire family in 1918 during the Russian Revolution.

ANATOLE—**m** 'Like the rising sun' (Greek). Anatole France (1844-1924), French writer and Nobel prizewinner.

ANCEL—**m** 'God-like' (Teutonic). Favourite name among the Normans.

ANDRA—**f** Form of Andrew.

ANDRAS—**m** Welsh form of Andrew.

ANDRÉ—**m** French form of Andrew. André Previn (born 1929), conductor.

ANDREA—**f** or **m** Feminine form of Andrew, but used in Italian for men, as Andrea del Sarto (1486-1531), Florentine painter.

ANDREANA—**f** Form of Andrew.

ANDREAS—**m** (Greek) Form of Andrew.

ANDRÉE—**f** French feminine form of Andrew. Modern English use dispenses with accent.

ANDREINA—**f** Form of Andrea.

ANDROULLA—**f** 'Womanly'. A form of Andrew.

ANDREW—**m** 'Manly' (Greek). First disciple called by Jesus. Martyred on an X-shaped cross, which is his symbol as the patron saint of Scotland.

ANDRIANA—**f** A modern invented name possibly from Andrew and Ariana.

ANDRINE—**f** Modern feminine form of Andrew.

ANDROCLES—**m** 'Glorious man' (Greek). *Androcles and the Lion* (1912), one of George Bernard Shaw's more popular plays.

ANEURIN—**m** A Welsh poet (AD *c*.600). The name is probably derived from the Latin Honorius. Aneurin Bevan (1897-1960), socialist politician.

ANGANAA—**f** 'Beautiful girl' (Hindu).

ANGEL—**m** 'Messenger' (Greek). Tess's husband in Hardy's *Tess of the D'Urbervilles* (1891). Common in Italy as Angelo.

ANGELA—**f** Form of Angel. Late nineteenth-century popularity, originally used for girls born about 29th September, the feast of St Michael and All Angels.

ANGELICA—**f** 'Like an angel' (Latin). Painter Angelica Kauffmann (1741-1807) was first female member of the Royal Academy.

ANGELINA—**f** Italian diminutive of Angela.

ANGELINE—**f** French form of Angelina.

ANGELIQUE—**f** French form of Angelica.

ANGHARAD—**f** 'Much loved one' (Welsh). Post-war revival of ancient name. Angharad Rees, television and stage actress.

ANGIE—**f** Affectionate form of Angela in use since the Second World War.

ANGUS—**m** 'Virtuous' (Gaelic). A thane of Scotland in Shakespeare's *Macbeth*. One of three Irish brothers who conquered Scotland, gave his name to the county and subsequently to the breed of cattle.

ANGWEN—**f** 'Beauteous' (Welsh).

ANIKA—**f** Possibly 'Sweetness of face' (Hausa). Slave name in the eighteenth century.

ANIMA—**f** 'Little darling' (Hindu).

ANITA—**f** Diminutive of Anne. Anita Brookner (born 1928),

author of *Hotel du Lac* and other novels.

ANITRA—**f** Coined by Henrik Ibsen for the name of an eastern princess in *Peer Gynt* (1867).

ANJUM—**m** 'Popular' (Hindu).

ANKE—**f** German pet form of Anne.

ANN, ANNE, ANNA—**f** English form of Hebrew Hannah, meaning 'Grace'. St Anne or Anna was the traditional mother of the Virgin Mary. Six English queens have borne the name.

ANNABEL, ANNABELLA—**f** Apparently a Scottish variant of Amabel, though by implication it can mean 'beautiful Anna'. The poem 'Annabel Lee' by Edgar Allan Poe (1849) may have spread its use.

ANNEKA—**f** See Annika. Anneka Rice, television personality.

ANNELIESE—**f** An invented name from Anne and Liese.

ANNELLA—**f** Scottish form of Anne.

ANNETTE—**f** French diminutive of Anne.

ANNICE—**f** Variant of Annis.

ANNIKA—**f** Swedish pet form of Anne.

ANNIS—**f** Form of Agnes.

ANNO—**m** Form of Arnold.

ANNONA—**f** 'Harvest' (Latin).

ANNORA—**f** 'Grace' (Hebrew). Annora Spence, contemporary British artist.

ANSARI—**m** 'Helper' (Arabic).

ANSELM—**m** May mean 'divinely helmeted' (Teutonic). St Anselm (1033-1109), Archbishop of Canterbury.

ANSTEY—**m** 'Resurrection' (Greek). Also an English surname and place-name meaning 'narrow path'.

ANTHEA—**f** 'Like a flower' (Greek). Robert Herrick (1591-1674) wrote the poem 'To Anthea, Who May Command Him Anything'.

ANTHONY—**m** May mean 'inestimable' (Latin). Often without the H. Name of the great Roman family that included Mark Antony. St Antony, patron saint of swineherds, established the first monastery in Christian history, *c.*300.

ANTIGONE—**f** 'Contrary birth' (Greek). Tragic daughter of Oedipus in Greek legend.

ANTOINE—**m** French form of Anthony.

ANTON—**m** German form of Anthony. Anton Bruckner (1824-96), Austrian composer.

ANTONIA, ANTOINETTE—**f** Italian and French diminutives of Anthony. Marie Antoinette, queen of Louis XVI, was guillotined in 1793.

ANTONINA—**f** Latin diminutive of Anthony.

ANTONY—**m** See under Anthony.

ANUKA—**f** 'So desired' (Hindu).

ANWYL—**m** 'Dear' (Welsh).

APHRA—**f** 'Dust' (Hebrew). Due to a Bible translator's error in the book of Micah, the word for dust was translated as a person's name. Aphra Behn (1640-89), English dramatist and novelist.

APHRODITE—**f** 'Foam-born' (Greek). The Grecian Venus.

APOLLONIA—**f** 'Sunny' (Latin). From Apollo, the Greek sun-god.

APRIL—**f** Example of the fashion for calling a child by the name of the month in which it was born.

AQUILA—**m** 'Eagle' (Latin). In early times used equally for both sexes.

ARABEL, ARABELLA—**f** (Latin). Late eighteenth-century romantic name.

ARAMINTA—**f** Seventeenth-century invention by Sir John Vanbrugh (1664-1726).

ARCHER—**m** Modern English derivation from the surname.

ARCHIBALD—**m** 'Genuine and bold' (Teutonic).

ARDAL—**m** 'Great valour' (Irish).

ARDATH—**f** 'Flowery meadow' (Hebrew).

AREL—**m** 'Man of God' (Hebrew).

ARIADNE—**f** 'Very holy' (Greek). Daughter of Minos, king of Crete, in Greek mythology. An asteroid (number 43) discovered in 1857.

ARIANA—**f** Derived from Ariadne.

ARIANWEN—**f** Possibly translated from the Welsh as 'beauty of the moon'. A daughter of the fifth-century Welsh tribal chief Brychan.

ARIEL—**m** Said to mean 'lion of God' in Hebrew, but best known as the spirit in Shakespeare's *The Tempest* who sings 'Where the bee sucks there suck I …'

ARLENE—**f** Short form variant of Adeline.

ARLETTE—**f** Mother of William the Conqueror.

ARMAND, ARMINEL—**m** Variants of Herman.

ARMSTRONG—**m** From the surname, self-explanatory.

ARNO—**m** Short form of Arnold. Also the river that flows through Florence.

ARNOLD—**m** 'Eagle-strength' (Teutonic). Came over with William the Conqueror, fell almost out of use, then came back strongly, perhaps through Thomas Arnold (1795-1842), headmaster of Rugby, and his son Matthew Arnold (1822-88), critic, poet and essayist. Arnold Bennett (1867-1931), novelist of the 'Five Towns' series.

ARON—**m** A variant of Aaron.

ARONA—**f** Derivation uncertain, possibly feminine form of Aron.

15

ART—**m** A diminutive of Arthur, now used independently.

ARTEMIS, ARTEMISIA—**f** Artemis (Diana in Latin) was the daughter of Zeus and goddess of hunting in Greek mythology. Artemisia was the name of her feast. Artemisia was also the queen who built the first mausoleum – in memory of her husband Mausolus, at Halicarnassus, about the fourth century BC.

ARTHUR—**m** 'High' (Celtic). The Arthurian legend gave it currency from early times. Popularised by the successes of Arthur Wellesley, Duke of Wellington, by Tennyson's *Idylls of the King*, retelling the legend, and by the fact that Queen Victoria chose it for her youngest son.

ARVAD—**m** 'The wanderer' (Hebrew).

ASA—**m** 'Good health' (Hebrew). King of Judah.

ASAPH—**m** 'Collector' (Hebrew). Appears in the Bible, the earliest reference being 2 Kings 18:18. Asaph Hall (1829-1907), American astronomer who discovered two satellites of Mars.

ASHER—**m** 'Happy' (Hebrew).

ASHLEY—**m** or **f** From surname via place-name, meaning 'ash copse' (Old English).

ASHTON—**m** Surname/place-name meaning 'ash town' (Old English).

ASIA—**f** One of the modern adoptions of names of continents and countries.

ASPASIA—**f** 'Welcome' (Greek). Mistress of Pericles (*c.*440 BC). Heroine of Beaumont and Fletcher's *The Maid's Tragedy* (1619).

ASSUNTA—**f** From the Italian title of the Virgin Mary, Maria Assunta, referring to her assumption into heaven.

ASTON—**m** Surname/place-name derivation (see Ashton). Sir Aston Webb (1849-1930), President of Royal Academy and architect.

ASTRID—**f** 'Divinely beautiful' (Old Norse). Much used by Scandinavian royalty from Canute onwards.

ATALANTA—**f** 'Legend' (Greek). The huntress who would marry only a man who could beat her in the famous foot-race.

ATARAH—**f** 'Crown' (Hebrew). One of the wives of Jerahmeel mentioned in the Bible (I Chronicles 2: 26).

ATHANASIA—**f** 'Immortal' (Greek). Feminine form of Athanasius.

ATHANASIUS—**m** 'Immortal' (Greek). St Athanasius (*c.*296-373) was one of the 'fathers' of the early church and is credited with writing a version of the Christian Creed.

ATHELSTAN—**m** 'Noble jewel' (Old English). King of Wessex from 925 to 939.

ATHENA, ATHENE—**f** The Greek goddess of wisdom and war (Minerva in Latin). She was worshipped at the Acropolis in Athens and later became patron of learning and the arts.

ATHERTON—**m** Surname/place-name meaning 'Athelhere's town' (Old English).

ATHOL—**m** or **f** Scottish place-name derivation.

ATYAANANDA—**m** 'Intense joy' (Hindu).

AUBERON—**m** A Norman French name, from 'Noble and bear-like' (Teutonic). Auberon Waugh (born 1939), author. A variant is Oberon.

AUBREY—**m** 'Wise ruler' (Old French, from Teutonic). Equivalent of Alberic.

AUDE—**m** French version of Alda, used in England in the twelfth century.

AUDREY—**f** Variant of Etheldreda. At St Etheldreda's (St Audrey's) Fair in the sixteenth century, cheap necklaces were sold, giving rise to 'tawdry' as a description of cheap, garish goods.

AUGUSTA—**f** Form of Augustus. For girls born in August.

AUGUSTINE—**m** Diminutive of Augustus. St Augustine of Hippo (354-430), a 'father' of the early church. Also another St Augustine, first Archbishop of Canterbury (601). The order of Augustin or Austin Friars instituted in the latter's name became the greatest sheep farmers in England. Thomas Augustine Arne (1710-78), composer of 'Rule, Britannia'.

AUGUSTUS—**m** 'Venerable' (Latin). Used by German princes after the Reformation in imitation of Roman emperors. Augustus Toplady, clergyman, composer of 'Rock of Ages' (*c*.1776).

AURELIA—**f** 'Golden' (Latin). Roman family name. Charmingly translated by an earlier writer on names as 'little pretty golden lady'.

AURORA—**f** 'Dawn' (Latin). Could refer to a baby born at daybreak.

AUSTIN—**m** Form of Augustine.

AVA—**f** Manufactured modern name, possibly for film star Ava Gardner (1922-90).

AVERIL—**f** 'Wild-boar battle' or 'wild boar protection' (Teutonic). Often confused with Avril, French for April.

AVERY—**f** Surname derivation or possibly popularisation of Averil.

AVICE—**f** From a Roman family name; also a variant of Avis.

AVIS—**f** 'War refuge' (Teutonic). In Latin, *avis* also means 'bird'.

AVRIL—**f** 'April' (French). Used for girls born in this month.

AXEL—**m** Scandinavian form of Absalom.

AYESHA—**f** 'Mother of the believers' (Arabic). Child-wife and favourite of Mohammed (*c*.611-78).

AYLMER—**m** 'Noble and famous' (Old English). Gave rise to the American form of Elmer.

AYLWIN—**m** 'Elf friend' or 'wise friend' (Old English).

AZARIAH—**m** 'Helped by God' (Hebrew).

BABER—**m** 'Lion' (Turkish). From 'Barbar', one of the names of the first Mogul ruler of India, *c*.1482-1530.

BABETTE—**f** French diminutive of Elizabeth.

BABS—**f** Affectionate short form of Barbara.

BACHIR—**m** 'Welcome' (Arabic).

BAILEY—**m** From the surname, meaning 'bailiff', or the place-name meaning 'berry field'.

BALABHADRA—**m** 'Strength and good fortune' (Hindu) – a name of Balder, brother of Krishna.

BALDRED—**m** 'Bold counsel' (Teutonic). Baldred was an early bishop of Glasgow.

BALDRIC—**m** 'Bold ruler' (Teutonic).

BALDWIN—**m** 'Brave friend' (Teutonic).

BALRAJ—**m** 'Strongest' (Hindi).

BALTHASAR—**m** 'Wise in battle' (Persian). The name given, by popular account, to one of the Three Wise Men. No fewer than five Shakespeare characters.

BAMBER—**m** Family name used in the Gascoigne family as a forename since the eighteenth century.

BAPTISTE—**m** 'Baptist' (French). Used in the form Jean-Baptiste, after the St John who baptised Christ.

BARAK—**m** 'Flash of lightning' (Hebrew).

BARBARA—**f** 'Stranger' (Greek). The legend of the virgin martyr St Barbara tells how her father imprisoned her in a tower to discourage suitors. After becoming a Christian, she lived as a hermit in a bath-house with three windows in honour of the Holy Trinity.

BARCLAY—**m** Scottish place-name/surname derivation. Walter de Berchelai, Chamberlain of Scotland 1165.

BARDOLPH—**m** 'Cunning wolf' (Teutonic). Falstaff's companion in three of Shakespeare's plays.

BARI—**m** 'The Maker' (Arabic).

BARNABAS, BARNABY—**m** 'Consoling son' (Hebrew). St Paul's travelling companion stoned to death as a martyr. *Barnaby Rudge* by Charles Dickens.

BARNET—**m** Place-name/surname derivation.

BARRETT—**m** Modern use of the surname.

BARRY—**m** 'Spear' (Irish). Also a short form of Finbar. Thackeray's *Barry Lyndon* is the story of an Irish rogue.

BART—**m** Short form of Bartholomew.

BARTHOLOMEW—**m** 'Son of Talmai' (Hebrew). Ancestral name of the apostle Nathaniel. St Bartholomew's Hospital founded by Rahere, court jester to Henry I, who claimed to have been cured through a vision of the saint.

BARTON—**m** Modern use of the surname from the place-name, meaning 'corn farm' or 'demesne farm' (Old English).

BARUCH—**m** 'Blessed' (Hebrew).

BASANT—**m** 'Spring' (Hindu), remembering the season of birth.

BASIL—**m** 'Kingly' (Greek). St Basil the Great (329-79) was one of the fathers of the early church.

BASILLA, BASILIA—**f** Form of Basil.

BASIMA—**f** 'Smiling' (Arabic).

BASTIAN—**m** Short form of Sebastian.

BAT—**m** Short form of Bartholomew.

BATHSHEBA—**f** 'Voluptuous' (Hebrew). The wife of Uriah and later the wife of David and mother of Solomon. Bathsheba Everdene, heroine of Thomas Hardy's *Far from the Madding Crowd* (1874).

BATYAH—**f** 'Daughter of God' (Hebrew). A variant of Bithiah, the Egyptian princess in I Chronicles 4:18.

BAXTER—**m** 'Baker' (Old English). Early surname.

BAZ—**m** Shortened form of Barry or Basil used in its own right.

BEA—**f** Short form of Beatrice. Bea Lilley (Beatrice Gladys), Lady Robert Peel (1898-1989), Canadian actress and entertainer.

BEAT—**m** Derived from the Latin for 'blessed'. Swiss hermit from whose lonely cell Beatanberg, Switzerland, grew.

BEATA—**f** 'Blessed' (Latin).

BEATHAN—**m** 'Life' (Gaelic).

BEATRICE, BEATRIX—**f** 'Bringer of joy' (Latin). Alternative derivation is from Latin *viatrix* meaning in this context 'voyager through life'. Beatrice is a main character in Shakespeare's *Much Ado About Nothing*. Dante's guide through Paradise in his *Divine Comedy* was Beatrice. Beatrix Potter (1866-1943), author of the 'Peter Rabbit' children's books.

BEAU—**m** 'Handsome' (French). Originally a nickname, as in Beau Brummell (1778-1840), Georgian dandy, Beau Geste in

P. C. Wren's book of that name (1924), and Beau Wilks, a character in Margaret Mitchell's *Gone with the Wind* (1936).

BEAUREGARD—**m** 'Beautiful look' (French).

BECKY—**f** Short form of Rebecca. Becky Sharp is the central character in Thackeray's *Vanity Fair* (1848).

BEDELIA—**f** Variant of Bridget.

BEDWIN—**m** 'As the birch tree' (Welsh).

BEHIRA—**f** 'Brilliant' (Hebrew).

BELINDA—**f** 'Sinuous' (Teutonic). Heroine of Pope's *Rape of the Lock* (1714) and title of Maria Edgeworth's novel published 1801.

BELITA—**f** 'Beautiful' (Spanish, from Latin).

BELLA—**f** 'Beautiful' (Italian and Spanish). Also short form of Isabella.

BELLAMY—**m** 'Good friend' (French). From the surname.

BELLE—**f** 'Beautiful' (French).

BENA—**f** 'The wise one' (Hebrew). A hope for the future!

BENEDICT—**m** 'Blessed' (Latin). Occurs also as Bennett. St Benedict (490-542), founder of the Benedictine order. A long line of popes bore this name.

BENEDICTA—**f** Female form of Benedict. The Spanish form of Benita is used in the USA.

BENIGNO—**m** 'Kind' (Italian). Dijon Cathedral is dedicated to St Benigno, third-century martyr.

BENITA—**f** 'Blessed' (Spanish).

BENJAMIN—**m** 'Son of the right hand' (Hebrew). Youngest son of Jacob, by Rachel. Big Ben: bell named after Sir Benjamin Hall, Commissioner of Works when it was installed.

BENNETT—**m** 'Blessed'. Medieval English form of Benedict. Also a surname.

BENSON—**m** Medieval origin, 'son of Ben'.

BENTLEY—**m** 'Bent grass meadow' (Old English). From the surname.

BENVENUTO—**m** 'Welcome' (Italian). Benvenuto Cellini (1500-71), outstanding sculptor and metalworker.

BERENGARIA—**f** 'Spear-bearing' (Teutonic). Queen of Richard I (married 1191). Little used, but some girls were called after the great transatlantic liner of the name.

BERENICE—**f** 'Bringer of victory' (Greek). Known better in recent times in its short form of Bernice. Racine's *Bérenice* (1670) is founded on the story of the Roman emperor Titus and the Jewish princess Berenice.

BERKELEY—**m** Place-name, meaning 'birchwood' (Old English).

BERNADETTE—**f** Diminutive of Bernard. St Bernadette of Lourdes (1844-79). The name was revived through the novel about her, *Song of Bernadette* by Franz Werfel (1942), and the subsequent film.

BERNARD—**m** 'Tough as a bear' (Teutonic). St Bernard of Menthon (923-1008) founded the hospices which gave aid to travellers in the Alps. Patron saint of mountaineers.

BERNEEN—**f** Irish short form of Bernadette.

BERNICE—**f** Variant of Berenice.

BERRY—**f** One of the more recent fruit and flower names.

BERTHA—**f** 'Bright' (Old English). The mother of Charlemagne, known as 'Bertha Big-foot'. Revived in Victorian times. Big Bertha: long-range gun used by Germans to shell Paris in 1918.

BERTRAM—**m** 'Bright raven' (Teutonic).

BERTRAND—**m** 'Bright shield' (Teutonic). Bertrand Russell, third Earl Russell (1872-1970), 'the greatest philosopher of the twentieth century'.

BERYL—**f** The name of a precious stone, derived from a Greek word of unknown derivation.

BESS, BESSIE, BETSY, BETTY—**f** All variations of Elizabeth which have been used in their own right.

BETH—**f** Variant of Elizabeth made popular by character Beth March in Louisa M. Alcott's *Little Women* (1868).

BETHAN, BETHANY—**f** Used by Roman Catholics in honour of Mary of Bethany, sister of Martha and Lazarus. The place where Jesus stayed prior to his trial and crucifixion.

BETHIA—**f** 'Daughter of God' (Hebrew).

BETTINA—**f** Spanish and Italian diminutive of Elizabeth.

BEULAH—**f** 'Married' (Hebrew). Name applied to Israel by prophet Isaiah.

BEVERLEY—**m** or **f** Place-name meaning 'beaver stream' (Old English). Town in Yorkshire, or as Beverly from Beverly Hills, Los Angeles.

BEVIS—**m** 'Bow' (Teutonic). The hero of Richard Jefferies's *Bevis, the Story of a Boy* (1882).

BHAGAT—**m** 'Joy' (Arabic).

BHAMINI—**f** 'Beautiful girl' (Hindu).

BHASVAN—**m** 'Shining light' (Hindu).

BIANCA—**f** 'White' (Italian). Characters of this name appear in Shakespeare's *Othello* and *The Taming of the Shrew*. More recently the name has been popularised by the TV serial *Eastenders*.

BIBI—**f** 'The lady of the house' (Persian).

BIDDULPH—**m** 'Commanding wolf' (Teutonic). Also a place name, perhaps meaning 'by the mine' (Old English).

BIDDY—**f** Short form of Bridget.

BIRGIT, BIRGITTA—**f** (Swedish). Derived from Brighid, Irish for Bridget. St Birgitta (1304-73), patron saint of Sweden, where the name is very popular.

BLAIR—**m** 'Plain dweller' (Gaelic). Place-name/surname origin.

BLAISE—**m** (French). Originally from the Latin for 'lisping'.

BLAKE—**m** Originally an Old English nickname for a dark-haired or, conversely, a pale man. Became a surname and in modern times a forename.

BLANCHE—**f** 'White' (French). Charles Lamb wrote in 1808: 'Blanche is out of fashion.' The Italian form is Bianca.

BLEDDYN—**m** 'Little wolf' (Welsh).

BLODWEN—**f** 'White [or holy] flower' (Welsh).

BLOSSOM—**f** One of the Victorian flower names.

BLYTH—**m** 'Happy' (Old English). Blythe for a girl.

BO—**m** 'Householder' (Scandinavian). Also used in feminine form for Bo Derrick, American film star.

BOAZ—**m** 'Swiftness' (Hebrew). In the Bible Ruth marries Boaz.

BONAMY—**m** 'Good friend' (French).

BONAR—**m** 'Courteous' (Old French).

BONIFACE—**m** 'Well-doer' (Latin). A third-century saint and a line of popes from 418.

BONITA—**f** 'Pretty' (Spanish). Used in USA from Second World War.

BONNIE—**f** Derives from French *bonne*, 'good', but use in Scotland popularised it. Modern trend from a character in *Gone with the Wind* by Margaret Mitchell (1936).

BOOTH—**m** 'Herdsman' (Old English).

BORIS—**m** 'Fighter' (Russian). Kings of Bulgaria from the earliest times. Boris Godunov (1552-1605), the Tsar of Russia who proposed to Queen Elizabeth I, is the subject of plays and operas.

BOTOLF, BOTOLPH—**m** 'Commanding wolf' (Teutonic). St Botolf (died 680) is claimed to have introduced the Benedictine rule into England. St Botolf's Town, Lincolnshire, is now known as Boston.

BOYD—**m** Scottish place-name derivation.

BRAD—**m** 'Broad' (Old English), but gained popularity as a short form of Bradley or Bradford.

BRADEN—**m** 'Broad valley' (Old English).

BRADLEY—**m** 'Broad meadow' (Old English).

BRAHMA—**m** (Sanskrit) Name of the creator of the universe.

BRANWEN—**m** or **f** 'Beautiful raven' (Welsh).

BRENDA—**f** 'Firebrand' (Old English). Its spread is attributed to Scott's use of it for a major character in *The Pirate* (1821).

BRENDAN—**m** 'Stinking hair' or 'prince' (Old Irish). Sixth-century Irish saint. Brendan Behan (1923-64), Irish playwright who wrote *The Quare Fellow*.

BRENNA—**f** 'Raven-haired beauty' (Irish).

BRENT—**m** 'Burnt' (Old English).

BRETT—**m** 'Breton' or 'Briton' (Old English). Surname derivation. May also mean 'bright', from Old English *beorht*.

BRIAN—**m** 'Strong' (Celtic). Derivation and meaning uncertain. Perhaps Irish in association with their national hero Brian Boru (926-1014).

BRIANA, BRIANNA—**f** Form of Brian used for a girl as early as 1908.

BRIDGET—**f** 'The high one' (Celtic). Brighid was the fire goddess of the Celts. St Brighid, Irish saint (453-523).

BRIGHAM—**m** Surname and place-name derivation (Old English, meaning 'village by the bridge') used mostly in USA. Influenced by Brigham Young (1801-77), early leader of the Mormon faith.

BRINSLEY—**m** Place-name meaning 'Brun's meadow' (Old English). Richard Brinsley Sheridan (1751-1816), Irish playwright, wrote *The Rivals* and *The School for Scandal*.

BRIONY—**f** Alternative spelling of Bryony.

BRITANNIA—**f** The name of Britain in ancient geography. Used as a Christian name in the eighteenth century.

BRONWEN—**f** 'Of the white bosom' (Welsh).

BRUCE—**m** From the place-name Brieuse in Normandy. Robert the Bruce (1274-1329), king of Scotland.

BRUNELLA—**f** Diminutive form of Bruno.

BRUNO—**m** 'Brown' (Teutonic). There are four saints of this name. Bruno Walter (1876-1962), German-born American conductor.

BRYAN—**m** Alternative spelling of Brian.

BRYONY—**f** Flower name; climbing plant found in hedges.

BUCK—**m** Originally a nickname for a spirited young man, especially in USA. Buck Rogers was a character in western films.

BUCKLEY—**m** Surname derivation.

BUD, BUDDY—**m** First used for a friend, from baby-talk or Black American slang for 'brother'.

BYRNE—**m** 'Coat of arms' (Old English).

BYRON—**m** Derivation from surname, spread by fame of Lord Byron (1788-1824), the poet.

BYSSHE—**m** 'From the thicket' (Old English). Percy Bysshe Shelley (1792-1822), English poet.

CADE—**m** Surname origin. Popularised by character in Margaret Mitchell's *Gone with the Wind* (1936).

CADELL—**m** From Old Welsh which can be translated as 'little warrior'.

CADMUS—**m** 'Man from Cadmea [the citadel of Thebes]' (Greek).

CADOGAN—**m** 'Glory in battle' (Welsh). Personal name of several medieval Welsh rulers. Later a surname; now in favour again as a forename.

CADWALLADER—**m** 'Battle-leader' (Welsh). Used in Wales from the seventh century. More common in England as a surname.

CAESAR—**m** 'Hairy one' (Latin). Also the word for 'elephant' in the Punic language. Title borne by Roman emperors after Julius Caesar and later as Tsar and Kaiser by Russian and German rulers. Sometimes given to boys born by Caesarean section.

CAITLIN—**f** Irish Gaelic form of Catherine.

CALDER—**m** 'The brook' (Anglo-Saxon).

CALEB—**m** 'Impetuous' (Hebrew). Old Testament Hebrew leader.

CALISTA—**f** 'Fairest' (Greek).

CALLAN—**m** Modern invention, after television character.

CALLIOPE—**f** 'Spirit of poetry' (Greek).

CALVIN—**m** Surname origin. Jean Calvin (1509-64), French protestant theologian. Popular in USA: Calvin Coolidge (1872-1933) was thirtieth President.

CALYPSO—**f** 'She who conceals' (Greek). In Greek legend, a nymph who kept Odysseus on her island, Ogygia, for seven years; but more probably from the West Indian song form of improvised lyrics to a variable rhythm.

CAMERON—**m** 'Crooked nose' (Gaelic).

CAMILLA—**f** 'Attendant at a sacrifice' (Etruscan). Queen of the Volscians in Virgil's *Aeneid*. Fanny Burney's *Camilla, or a Picture of Youth* (1796) may have started its modern revival.

CAMPBELL—**m** From surname of one of the famous Highland clans of Scotland. Gaelic original referred to an ancestor with a 'crooked mouth'.

CANDICE—**f** Name of a succession of queens of Ethiopia, one of whom is mentioned in the Bible. Also spelt Candace.

CANDIDA—**f** 'White' (Latin). Given limited popularity by Shaw's play of that name in 1898.

CANDY—**f** Mostly used in USA implying 'sweet as candy'.

CANTARA—**f** 'Small bridge' (Arabic), implying the baby is the bridge between the parents.

CARA—**f** 'Dear' (Italian).

CARADOC—**m** 'Amiable' (Welsh). Equivalent of the old British name of Caractacus, British king, son of Cymbeline, who ruled at Colchester.

CAREEN—**f** Invented name used by Margaret Mitchell for a character in *Gone with the Wind* (1936).

CAREY—**m** From an Irish surname; also resembles the Irish Gaelic for 'of the dark one'.

CARILLA—**f** Alternative form of Carla.

CARINA—**f** 'Pretty' (Italian).

CARL—**m** An American compromise between the English Charles and the German Karl.

CARLA—**f** Feminine form of Carl. Carla Lane, television writer.

CARLOTTA—**f** Italian variant of Charlotte. Carlotta Grisi (1819-99), Italian romantic ballerina.

CARLY—**f** Diminutive form of Carla.

CARMEL—**f** 'Garden' or 'orchard' (Hebrew). Site where Elijah challenged the prophets of Baal. Mount Carmel, near modern Haifa, was the place of origin of the Carmelite religious order, *c.*1155.

CARMEN—**f** 'Song' (Latin). Opera (1875) by Bizet, based on novel by Prosper Mérimée.

CAROL, CAROLE—**f** 'Song' (French). Also a form of Charles and short form of Caroline, spreading from the southern United States.

CAROLA—**f** Form of Charles. Carola Oman, historical novelist.

CAROLINE—**f** From Carolina, Italian feminine form of Charles which spread to Germany and was introduced to England through the popularity of George II's Queen Caroline of Brandenburg-Anspach (1683-1737).

CAROLYN—**f** Form of Caroline.

CARRIE—**f** Affectionate form of Caroline.

CARROLL—**m** Anglicised from Irish Cearbhall.

CARSON—**m** or **f** Derivation from surname or place-name not now identifiable. Carson McCullers (1917-67), American novelist.

CARY—**m** or **f** May mean 'Pleasant stream'. British river name, possibly also relating to Welsh *caru* ('love'). Made popular through Cary Grant (1904-89), American film star.

CARYL—**f** 'The loved one' (Welsh).

CASEY—**m** or **f** Origin of male form uncertain. Female form may be alternative of Cassie.

CASIMIR—**m** 'Proclaimer of peace' (Polish). A line of Polish kings.

CASPAR—**m** 'Keeper of the treasure' (Persian). One of the Three Wise Men. Variants are Gasper, Jasper, Kaspar.

CASSANDRA—**f** Daughter of Priam, king of Troy, in Greek legend. Cursed by Apollo that, although her prophecies would be true, no one would believe her. Jane Austen's older sister was a bearer of the name.

CASSIDY—**m** 'Ingenious' (Celtic). Surname derivation.

CATALINA—**f** Spanish form of Catherine.

CATHAL—**m** 'Victor in battle' (Gaelic). Name of seventh-century saint, formerly head of Lismore Abbey school.

CATHERINE, CATHARINE—**f** 'Pure' (Greek). St Catherine of Alexandria, who was broken on a wheel and then beheaded in 307, is remembered in the Catherine wheel. St Catherine of Siena (c.1347-80) led an exemplary life of prayer and charity and was a great spiritual leader.

CATHLEEN—**f** Irish form of Catherine.

CAVAN—**m** 'Handsome' (Gaelic).

CECIL—**m** 'Blind' (Latin). Originally from the great Roman family Caecilius, but more recently from the family name of the influential Marquess of Salisbury. Cecil Rhodes (1853-1902), founder of Rhodesia.

CECILIA—**f** Form of Cecil. St Cecilia, martyred about 177, is patron saint of music and poetry. William the Conqueror's daughter Cecilia was abbess of Caen. Its later revival may be due to Fanny Burney's novel *Cecilia* (1782). Cecily, Cicely, Ciss and Cis are derivations and diminutives.

CEDRIC—**m** Apparently invented by Sir Walter Scott for one of his characters in *Ivanhoe* (1820). He may have meant Cerdic, founder of the West Saxon kingdom. The hero of *Little Lord Fauntleroy* (1886), by Frances Hodgson Burnett.

CEINWEN—**f** 'Blessed and lovely' (Welsh). Fifth-century saint, daughter of Welsh chief Brychan.

CELESTE—**f** 'Heaven sent' (Latin).

CELIA—**f** 'Heavenly' (Latin). A modern Italian version of the Roman family name, though the English form is more likely a diminutive of Cecilia. Cousin of Rosalind in Shakespeare's *As You Like It*. Popular in poetry, e.g. Ben Jonson's 'To Celia', better known as 'Drink to me only with thine eyes …'.

CERELIA—**f** 'Spring-like' (Latin). Implies 'spring-blossom beauty' of baby.

CERI—**m** 'Dear one' (Welsh). Ceri Richards (1903-71), Welsh artist.

CERIDWEN—**f** 'Fair poetry' (Welsh). Welsh goddess of poetry.

CHAD—**m** 'Battle' (Celtic). St Chad (died 672) founded the diocese of Lichfield. Perhaps popularised, particularly in USA, by Walter Edmonds's circus story hero, Chad Hanna.

CHANDANI—**f** 'Moonlight' (Hindu).

CHANDAR—**m** 'Born when the moon was shining' (Sanskrit).

CHANTAL—**f** 'Stone' or 'boulder'(Old Provençal). St Jeanne of Chantal (1572-1641) in her widowhood founded a new order of nuns.

CHANTELLE—**f** (French). A modern invention, probably appealing on sound alone.

CHARIS—**f** 'Grace' (Greek). In Greek mythology the wife of Hephaestus, personification of grace and beauty.

CHARISSA—**f** Modern hybrid of Charis and Clarissa.

CHARITY—**f** 'Love' (Latin). Names from qualities became fashionable after the Reformation. So Faith, Hope and Charity were often used for triplets. Early contracted into Cherry, as shown by the daughter of Mr Pecksniff in Dickens's *Martin Chuzzlewit* (1843).

CHARLENE—**f** Modern invention, popularised by the Australian soap opera *Neighbours.*

CHARLES—**m** 'A man' (Teutonic). Popular through the exploits of Charles the Great, otherwise Charlemagne. Ten French and fifteen Swedish rulers have borne this name. In England supporters of Charles I and Charles II gave it wide circulation. Prince Charles, Prince of Wales, born 14th November 1948, is the heir to the British throne.

CHARLOTTE—**f** Form of Charles. George III's marriage to Charlotte Sophia of Mecklenburg-Strelitz made it popular. Charlotte Brontë (1816-55), author of *Jane Eyre*. The late Queen Salote of Tonga showed the name in its local form.

CHARLTON—**m** Derived from a place-name meaning 'town of free peasants'. Charlton Heston (born 1923), film actor.

CHARMAINE—**f** In use since 1920, repopularised by the Bachelors' hit song of the 1960s.

CHARMIAN—**f** 'A little joy' (Greek). Shakespeare chose it for a character in *Antony and Cleopatra* (1608).

CHARVAK—**m** 'Beautiful' (Sanskrit).

CHAUNCEY—**m** USA adoption of the surname, perhaps from Charles Chauncy (1592-1672), President of Harvard College.

CHELLE—**f** A short pet form of Michelle.

CHELSEA—**f** Recent popular use of the place-name (meaning 'chalk wharf'). Chelsea Clinton, daughter of the American President.

CHERELLE—**f** A new way of using Cheryl with a French-type ending.

CHERIE—**f** 'Beloved' (French). Cherie Booth, wife of Tony Blair, British Prime Minister from 1997.

CHERISH—**f** Modern introduction implying value of child to parents.

CHERRY—**f** Anglicised form of *Chérie*, French for 'darling', but also intended to express the beauty of cherry blossom. Dickens's *Martin Chuzzlewit* (1843) has Mr Pecksniff's daughter called Cherry as a pet-form of Charity.

CHERYL—**f** 'Love' (Welsh).

CHESTER—**m** Place-name derivation.

CHIARA—**f** Italian form of Clara. Pronounced 'Kiara'.

CHLOE—**f** 'Blooming' (Greek). One of the titles of Ceres or Demeter, goddess of harvest and abundance.

CHLORIS—**f** 'Leaf green' (Greek). Goddess of flowers, whom the Romans called Flora.

CHRISTA—**f** Shortened form of Christine now used in its own right.

CHRISTABEL—**f** 'Fair Christian' (Latin). Heroine of the Middle English ballad of the brave knight Sir Cauline, and also of S. T. Coleridge's *Christabel* (1816). Dame Christabel Pankhurst, women's suffrage leader, daughter of Emmeline Pankhurst.

CHRISTELLE—**f** Variant of Christine, possibly influenced by use of Crystal.

CHRISTIAN—**m** 'A Christian' (Latin). Its occurrence may have been influenced by the hero of Bunyan's *Pilgrim's Progress* (1678). Ten Danish kings were so called.

CHRISTINE, CHRISTINA—**f** Form of Christian. St Christina, martyred 295, was a high-born Roman. Christina Rossetti (1830-94), poet.

CHRISTMAS—**m** Obviously from the great Christian festival.

CHRISTOPHER—**m** 'Bearing Christ' (Latin). Legend tells how St Christopher, an early Christian martyr, carried the infant Christ across a river; for this reason he became the patron saint of travellers. For early Christians, however, the name would have signified bearing Christ in their hearts.

CHRISTY—**m** or **f** Derived from the surname or a diminutive of Christopher.

CHRYSANDER—**m** 'Golden man' (Greek).

CHRYSOGON—**f** 'Golden women' (Greek). Variants like Grisogon date from the earliest times.

CIARA—**f** (Irish). Modern form of Ciarán.

CIARÁN—**m** 'Little dark one' (Irish Gaelic).

CICELY—**f** Form of Cecilia. Also a plant name, as in sweet cicely.

CINDY—**f** Short form of Cinderella which gave rise to the 'Sindy' play doll, complete with all its accoutrements, so popular from 1960s onwards. Could also be a pet form of Lucinda or Cynthia.

CLAIRE—**f** 'Bright'. French form of Clare. Actress Claire Bloom.

CLARA, CLARE—**f** 'Bright' (Latin). St Clare of Assisi (1194-1253) was founder of the Order of Poor Clares and proclaimed by Pope Pius XII as patron saint of television in 1958.

CLARENCE—**m** From the dukedom of Clarence created in 1362 for Lionel, third son of Edward III, who married the heiress of Clare in Suffolk.

CLARETTE—**f** English diminutive of Clare, using a French ending.

CLARIBEL—**f** 'Brightly fair' (Latin). Queen of Tunis in Shakespeare's *The Tempest*.

CLARICE—**f** A French version of Clare.

CLARIMOND—**f** 'Famous protector', from a joint Latin and Teutonic derivation. A further development of Clara, used in Old French romances.

CLARINDA—**f** Version of Clara. Popular name for a character in early drama.

CLARISSA—**f** Developed from the French form of Clare. *Clarissa Harlowe* by Samuel Richardson (1747) popularised the name.

CLARK—**m** 'Clerk' (Latin). In the middle ages the word meant a scholar or cleric. Surname derivation.

CLAUD—**f** 'Lame' (Latin). From Claudius, name of two great Roman families.

CLAUDETTE—**f** French female diminutive of Claud.

CLAUDIA—**f** Form of Claud, common in Roman times.

CLAUDINE—**f** French diminutive of Claudia. Subject of a series of novels by Colette.

CLAUS—**m** (German) Short form of Nicholas. Affectionately associated with St Nicholas (Santa Claus), which inhibits its regular use.

CLAY—**m** Use of an old English surname. Clay Jones, broadcaster on gardening topics in 1980s and 1990s.

CLEDWYN—**m** 'Rough but fair' (Welsh).

CLEMENCE—**f** 'Mildness' (Latin).

CLEMENT—**m** 'Mild' (Latin). Name of a saint, who was pope 88-97, beginning a line of fourteen popes. St Clement Danes church was built for Danish settlers in London, for whom St Clement was significant as patron saint of sailors and blacksmiths.

CLEMENTINE—**f** Form of Clement. Heroine of the song, 'O my darling Clementine'.

CLEO—**f** Short form of Cleopatra. Cleo Lane, jazz singer.

CLEOPATRA—**f** The famous Egyptian queen (69-30 BC), renowned for her beauty and her love affairs.

CLIFF—**m** See Clifford; the shortened form made popular by Cliff Richard (Harry Webb), singer (born 1940).

CLIFFORD—**m** Classic example of a place-name evolving as a surname and then from late Victorian times as a Christian name.

CLIFTON—**m** Place-name derivation.

CLINT—**m** Short form of Clinton, made popular by film actor Clint Eastwood (born 1930).

CLINTON—**m** 'Town on a hill' (Old Norse/Old English). Name of at least ten places in the USA.

CLIONA—**f** A further diminutive of Cleopatra. Cliona Bacon, picture restorer after Windsor Castle fire of 1992.

CLIVE—**m** From the Shropshire place-name meaning 'cliff'.

CLODAGH—**f** (Irish). Recent introduction from the river in Tipperary.

CLOTILDA—**f** 'in battle' or 'loud in battle' (Teutonic). The wife of Clovis, king of France (465-511), whom she successfully persuaded to embrace Christianity.

CLOVER—**f** From the sweet-smelling clover flower.

CLOVIS—**m** 'Loud in victory' (Teutonic). Clovis, Merovingian king of France (465-511).

CLYDE—**m** Scottish river derivation.

COLBERT—**m** Obscure derivation, possibly linked to the Teutonic word for 'bright' or the Latin *libertus,* 'free'. Introduced by Normans as a forename, became a surname, now used as a forename again.

COLETTE—**f** Diminutive of the French Nicole. St Colette, died 1447, founded seventeen convents of the Coletine Poor Clares. 'Colette', pseudonym of the French novelist (1873-1954).

COLIN—**m** 'Youth' (Gaelic). An abbreviation of Nicholas, originating in France but used in England from the thirteenth century.

COLLEEN—**f** 'Girl' (Gaelic). Not used as a given name in Ireland but was especially popular in USA during the 1940s.

COLLEY—**m** Nickname for a swarthy person. Colley Cibber (1671-1757), English actor.

COLMAN—**m** 'Dove' (Irish). Several early Irish saints bear this name.

COLUMBA—**f** 'The dove' (Latin). After the male St Columba (*c.* 521-97), Irish-born abbot and missionary who founded a monastery on Iona, an island off the west coast of Scotland.

COLUMBINE—**f** Flower name used from Victorian times. Also a stock character from the *Commedia dell' arte*, an Italian-derived dramatic form.

COMFORT—**f** Obvious derivation.

CONAL, CONALL—**m** 'Powerful potentate' (Celtic).

CONAN—**m** 'High' (Celtic). One of the early bishops of London. Sir Arthur Conan Doyle (1859-1930), creator of Sherlock Holmes.

CONCEPTA—**f** (Latin). Refers to the Immaculate Conception of the Virgin Mary. Used chiefly in Ireland by Roman Catholics.

CONNIE—**f** Short form of Constance.

CONNOR—**m** 'High desire' (Irish).

CONRAD—**m** 'Bold counsel' (Teutonic). Joseph Conrad (1857-

1924), Polish-born English novelist who adopted the name for his first novel when he was thirty-seven.

CONSTANCE—**f** 'Steadfastness' (Latin). A saint who was the daughter of Constantine the Great. One of the 'virtue' names popular in the nineteenth century.

CONSTANTINE—**m** 'Persevering' (Latin). Constantine the Great (274-337), first Roman emperor to give official recognition to Christianity.

CORA, CORE—**f** 'Girl' (Greek). Dryden uses Corah in 'Absalom and Achitophel' in 1681. Cora is also the heroine of J. F. Cooper's *Last of the Mohicans* (1826).

CORAL—**f** One of the 'precious stone' names common in the 1920s.

CORALIE—**f** Modern development of Cora.

CORDELIA—**f** 'Jewel of the sea' (Celtic). Best known from the tragic character in Shakespeare's *King Lear*.

CORETTA—**f** Diminutive of Cora. Name of the widow (born 1927) of Martin Luther King, American politician and civil-rights worker.

COREY—**m** Surname derivation used mostly in USA.

CORINNA, CORINNE—**f** Diminutive of Cora. Corinna was a fifth-century BC Greek lyric poet whose name was used by Robert Herrick and other seventeenth-century poets. The second, French, form is more popular today.

CORISANDE—**f** Originates in a medieval romance. Disraeli used it for a character in his *Lothair*.

CORMAC—**m** (Gaelic). Traditional and popular Irish name from as far back as a tenth-century king.

CORNELIA—**f** Form of Cornelius. Cornelia, a Roman matron of the second century BC, was celebrated for her accomplishments and virtues as a mother.

CORNELIUS—**m** 'Horned' (Latin). The great Roman family name which included Scipio. The name of the centurion converted by St Peter.

CORNELL—**m** Form of Cornelius made popular by the American university.

COSIMA—**f** Feminine form of Cosmo. Cosima Wagner (1837-1930), daughter of Franz Liszt and wife of Richard Wagner.

COSMO, COSIMO—**m** 'Order' (Greek). Cosimo de Medici (1519-74), Grand Duke of Tuscany.

COSTIN—**m** Modern form of Constantine.

COURTENAY—**m** Place-name in the Ile de France which evolved via a surname.

COURTNEY—**m** or **f** Use of the Norman baron's surname derived from the French place-name.

CRAIG—**m** 'Crag' (Gaelic).

CRESSA—**f** Modern short form of Cressida.

CRESSIDA—**f** Loosely based on the Greek *khrysos,* 'gold'. Complicated derivation through the Troilus and Cressida legend, from Boccaccio through Chaucer to Shakespeare.

CRISPIN—**m** 'With the curly hair' (Latin). St Crispin, patron saint of shoemakers and one of two brothers martyred in 287. His day is 25th October, the date of the battle of Agincourt.

CRISTO—**m** (Spanish). Short form of Cristobál but also used in its own right. Can also be an abbreviation of Christopher.

CRYSTAL—**f** Developed alongside the modern gem names, but could have been influenced by the Crystal Palace put up for the 1851 Great Exhibition in London.

CURRAN—**m** 'Hero' (Celtic).

CURTIS—**m** From the surname. A serving man in Shakespeare's *The Taming of the Shrew*.

CUTHBERT—**m** 'Famous and bright' (Old English). The body of St Cuthbert (died 687), preserved in Durham Cathedral, was reputed to have worked miracles. In the First World War the name was used to describe those who evaded conscription.

CY—**m** Short form of Cyrus, originating from USA.

CYNDA—**f** Probably made up from Cynthia.

CYNTHIA—**f** 'Of Mount Cynthos' (Greek). Poet's name for Queen Elizabeth I. Character in Mrs Gaskell's *Wives and Daughters* (1865).

CYPRIAN—**m** 'Of Cyprus' (Latin). St Cyprian, martyred at Carthage in 258.

CYRIL—**m** 'Lordly' (Greek). There were at least three saints of this name up to the ninth century, but it has been fashionable in Britain only since the late nineteenth century.

CYRUS—**m** 'Throne' (Persian). Cyrus the Great, the founder of the Persian empire, figures prominently in the Bible (died 529 BC). General Cyrus Choke was a remarkable American featured in Dickens's *Martin Chuzzlewit* (1843).

DACRE—**m** Though originally inferring 'a man from Acre in Palestine', it is derived today from the great English family name.

DAFFODIL—**f** Modern flower name.

DAGMAR—**f** (Scandinavian). Interpretation difficult. Could be from a Slavonic name meaning 'dear and famous'. Given some English recognition through the rose 'Frau Dagmar Hastrup'.

DAGNY—**f** 'New day' (Scandinavian).

DAGOBERT—**m** 'Day-bright' (Old English).

DAHAB—**m** 'Gold' (Arabic).

DAHLIA—**f** From the striking late-summer flower named after the Swedish botanist Anders Dahl (1751-89).

DAI—**m** 'Shining' (celtic). A name in its own right, though mostly used as a Welsh short form of David.

DAISY—**f** Flower name. Originally a pet-name for Margaret in Victorian times.

DALE—**m** 'Valley' (Old English).

DALEY—**m** Derivation from the English surname.

DAMARIS—**f** Probably from Greek *damar,* 'wife'. Through confusion with Greek *damalis* it has been taken to mean 'a young cow'! New Testament woman converted by St Paul.

DAMIAN, DAMON—**m** 'Tamer' (Greek).

DANA—**f** Celtic goddess of fertility.

DANE—**f** Surname and place-name (Dean) variation through dialect pronunciation.

DANIEL—**m** 'Whom God has judged' (Hebrew). Hero of the lions' den. Daniel Defoe (1660-1731), novelist and political journalist famous for *Robinson Crusoe*.

DANIELA—**f** Polish and Czech Latinate form of Daniel.

DANIELE—**f** (French). Feminine of Daniel, also spelt Danielle, Daniela.

DANIKA—**f** 'Morning star' (Slavonic). Spreading to England from eastern Europe.

DANNI—**f** Short form of Daniele, with a light-hearted spelling.

DANUTA—**f** (Polish). Meaning uncertain, possibly a variant of Dana or Donata.

DAPHNE—**f** 'Laurel' (Greek). A nymph loved by Apollo and turned into a bush. Now used for a range of flowering shrubs.

DARA—**f** 'Wisdom and charity' (Hebrew).

DARBY—**m** 'Never envious' (Old Irish). A debased form of Diarmit which may have given rise to the 'Darby and Joan' first celebrated in verse in 1735.

DARCY—**m** or **f** Family name (D'Arcy) of one of William I's Norman knights, remembered in the village of Tolleshunt D'Arcy, Essex.

DARIA—**f** Feminine form of Darius. Name of a saint who died in 283.

DARIUS—**m** 'Benevolent ruler' (Greek). From a line of ancient

Persian kings.

DARLENE, DARLINE, DARALYN—**f** Forms of Darrel.

DARREL(L), DARYL—**m** From the Norman surname d'Airelle. Darrell Fancourt (1888-1953) played the role of the Mikado in the Gilbert and Sullivan opera over three thousand times.

DARREN—**m** Recently introduced, of uncertain origin. The first mention found is of Darren McGavin, American actor, born 1922. Popularised by a character in American comedy television series *Bewitched*. Bobby Darin (1936-72), American singer, chose the name from a telephone directory.

DAVID—**m** 'Beloved' (Hebrew). David, the killer of Goliath, grew up to be second king of Israel. The patron saint of Wales (died 601), called Dafydd in Welsh.

DAVINA—**f** Latinised form of David; sometimes altered to Davinia.

DAWN—**f** A modern name from romantic writers.

DAYANITA—**f** 'Tender, loving' (Hindu).

DEAN—**m** 'Valley' (Teutonic). Surname used as forename.

DEANNA—**f** Modern variation of Diana. Deanna Durbin, popular singing film actress of 1940s.

DEBORAH—**f** 'A bee' (Hebrew). Later interpreted as 'eloquent'. A prophetess in biblical times (Judges 4). John Milton's youngest daughter.

DECIMA—**f** Form of Decimus.

DECIMUS—**m** 'Tenth' (Latin). Used in Victorian families for the tenth child. Decimus Burton (1800-81), architect, designer of the triumphal arch at Hyde Park Corner, London.

DECLAN—**m** (Irish) Uncertain origin. Made popular by television character of the 1990s.

DEE—**f** Short form of many forenames but now used independently. Also a river name.

DEIRDRE—**f** 'Fear' (Celtic). Much featured in Irish plays and poems.

DELANO—**m** 'Grove of alders' (Latin). Franklin Delano Roosevelt (1882-1945) was thirty-second President of the USA.

DELFINE—**f** 'Larkspur' – form of Delphine.

DELIA—**f** 'Of Delos' (Greek). Sometimes short for Cordelia.

DELIAN—**m** Origin unknown, but could be from Greek – Akenside described Apollo, or the sun, as the Delian king in 'Hymn to the Naiads' in 1767.

DELICIA—**f** 'Delight' (Latin). Recent origin has already given rise to Delice.

DELILAH—**f** 'Delight' (Hebrew). Delilah brought about the downfall of Samson in the Old Testament.

DELITE—**f** Modern invention to reflect the delight in the safe birth.

DELLA—**f** Diminutive of Adela or Delia.

DELMAR—**m** Unknown origin: possibly a variant of Elmer or from the Spanish for 'of the sea'.

DELORA—**f** 'From the seashore' (Latin).

DELPHINE—**f** 'Woman from Delphi' (Latin). Modern use may be from connection with the flower delphinium.

DELROY—**m** Origin uncertain. Could have French derivation, meaning 'of the king'. Popular with West Indians in Britain.

DELTA—**f** (Greek). Fourth letter of Greek alphabet, used for a fourth child.

DEMELZA—**f** (English). Used since 1950s, from Cornish place-name. Heroine of Winston Graham's *Poldark* novels.

DEMETRIA—**f** 'Fertility' (Greek), after the goddess.

DEMYAN—**m** Russian form of Damian.

DENA—**f** Modern invention, possibly variant of Dinah.

DENISE—**f** Borrowed from the French as a female version of Dennis.

DENNIS—**m** 'Of Dionysus' (Greek). The name of several saints. Sometimes spelt Denis.

DENTON—**m** Surname and place-name origin.

DENZIL—**m** Surname derivation. Denzil Holles (1599-1670), English statesman.

DEREK—**m** Derives from Theodoric. Sometimes spelt Derrick.

DERINA—**f** Form of Derwin.

DERMOT—**m** Derives from Diarmit.

DERWIN—**m** 'Sincere friend' (Old English).

DESDEMONA—**f** 'Misery' (Greek). The tragic heroine of Shakespeare's *Othello*.

DESIRÉE—**f** 'Desired' (French).

DESMOND—**m** 'South Munster' (Irish Gaelic). Evolved from a place-name and a surname.

DESNA—**f** Possibly a shortening of Desdemona, or a misreading of Desma, 'pledge' (Greek), which first appeared in the 1940s.

DEVDAN—**m** 'Gift of God'. Derived from Sanskrit Devadana.

DEVI—**f** 'Divine'. Hindu goddess, wife of Shiva.

DEVON—**m** Originally from the county name. Now popular in the USA. Devon Malcolm (born 1963), Jamaican-born British cricketer.

DEVORAH—**f** Modern Hebrew form of Deborah.

DEWI—**m** A Welsh form of David. St Dewi or David was born in south Wales in the fifth century.

DEXTER—**m** From the surname, which, in Old English, meant a female dyer. The name also means 'right-handed' or 'skilful' (Latin).

DHAVAL—**f** 'Purest white' (Hindu).

DIANA—**f** Diana (Artemis in Greek) was the daughter of Jupiter (Zeus) and the goddess of hunting. Became popular through the heroine of Scott's *Rob Roy* and Meredith's *Diana of the Crossways*, and made very popular by Diana, Princess of Wales, who died tragically in 1997.

DIANE—**f** French form of Diana.

DIARMIT—**m** 'Never envious' (Old Irish). The origin of Dermot and Darby.

DIDI—**f** 'Beloved' (Hebrew).

DIDO—**f** Queen of Carthage in Roman mythology.

DIETER—**m** 'People's warrior' (Teutonic).

DIETMAR—**m** 'Famous among people' (Teutonic).

DIGBY—**m** Place-name/surname, meaning 'farm at the ditch' (Old Norse).

DIGNA—**f** 'Worthy' (Latin).

DILLON—**m** From a surname of Norman origin.

DILWYN—**m** Welsh place-name.

DILYS—**f** 'Genuine' (Welsh). Dilys Powell, film critic and author.

DINAH—**f** 'Judgement' (Hebrew). Daughter of Jacob and Leah.

DIONYSIUS—**m** 'Of Dionysus' (Greek). Dionysus was the fertility god from whom the powerful tyrant of Syracuse (died 367 BC) got his name. It continued into Christian times as the name of a saint and pope. Its modern form is Dennis.

DIPAK—**m** 'Shining bright' (Sanskrit). Another name for Kama, the God of love. Also in the variant Deepak.

DIRK—**m** Dutch short form of Derek. Dirk Bogarde, actor (born 1921).

DIVYA—**f** 'Heavenly' (Hindi).

DODIE—**f** Short form of Dorothy. C. L. Anthony, playwright, novelist and author of children's book *The Hundred and One Dalmatians* (1956), wrote under the pseudonym of Dodie Smith.

DOLLY—**f** Pet name for Dorothy.

DOLORES—**f** 'Sorrows' (Spanish). Short for 'Mary of the Sorrows', i.e. the mother of Jesus.

DOMINIC—**m** 'Of the Lord' (Latin). Perhaps used in the sense 'of the Lord's Day', for boys born on a Sunday. St Dominic founded the order of preaching friars (*c.*1200) known as Black Friars from the colour of their habit.

DOMINICA—**f** Form of Dominic.

DONALD—**m** 'Proud chief' (Celtic). Common in Scotland, where it began. Reckoned to be the name of the first Christian king of Scotland.

DONATELLO, DONATELLA—**m** or **f** Diminutive forms of Donato.

DONATO, DONATA—**m** or **f** 'God-given' (Italian).

DONNA—**f** 'Woman' (Italian). Also modern feminine form of Donald and short form of Madonna.

DONOVAN—**m** (Irish) Surname origin. Folk and rock singer of 1960s, Donovan, may have made it popular.

DORA—**f** 'Gift' (Greek). Also short form of Dorothy.

DORCAS—**f** 'Gazelle' (Greek). In the New Testament (Acts 9: 36) Dorcas was a woman who made clothes for the poor.

DOREEN—**f** An adaptation Doirean, the Irish form of Dorothy. Its popularity may derive from Edna Lyall's novel *Doreen* (1894).

DORELIA—**f** Made up from the Irish for Doreen. Second wife of Augustus John, artist (1878-1961).

DORIAN—**m** Greek place-name derivation.

DORINDA—**f** Eighteenth-century romantic diminutive of Dorothy. The daughter of Lady Bountiful in Farquhar's *The Beaux' Stratagem* (1707).

DORIS—**f** The name of a sea nymph in Greek mythology. Noted by Dickens, it then became popular by 1900.

DOROTHY, DOROTHEA—**f** 'Gift of God' (Greek). Often abbreviated to Dolly and further to Doll – the word 'doll' only came to mean a child's toy as a result of the popularity of that name.

DOUGAL—**m** 'Black stranger' (Old Irish). Character in Scott's *Rob Roy*.

DOUGLAS—**m** 'Dark blue' (Celtic). Originally a river name which became the title of the great Scottish family.

DREDA—**f** 'Strength' (Old English). Short form of Etheldreda, used from the middle of the nineteenth century.

DRUSILLA—**f** Roman family name. Livia Drusilla (58 BC to AD 29) was the third wife of Augustus, and Herod named his daughter thus.

DUANE—**m** 'Little dark one' (Irish). Surname origin. Popular in the 1950s through singer-guitarist Duane Eddy. Also spelt Dwain, Dwayne.

DUDLEY—**m** A nineteenth-century compliment to the powerful Tudor family, whose surname derived from a place-name.

DUFF—**m** 'Black hair' (Gaelic).

DULCE, DULCI, DULCIE—**f** 'Sweet' (Latin).

DULCIBELLA—**f** 'Sweet and beautiful' (Latin).

DUNCAN—**m** 'Brown warrior' (Old Irish). Two Scottish kings of the eleventh century, the first murdered by Macbeth and immortalised by Shakespeare.

DUNSTAN—**m** 'Stone on a hill' or 'of the stony hill' (Old English). St Dunstan (924-88) became Archbishop of Canterbury and patron saint of goldsmiths.

DURAND—**m** 'Lasting' (Latin). Occasionally shown as Durant.

DURWYN—**m** Possibly from 'Durwan' (Hindustani adoption of Persian) meaning a porter or doorkeeper, anglicised as early as 1773.

DWIGHT—**m** Surname carried from England to America by early settlers, where it was borne by a long line of famous men and women and so became a forename, as in Dwight D. Eisenhower (1890-1969), thirty-fourth President of the USA.

DYLAN—**m** 'Son of the wave' (Welsh). Legendary hero. Dylan Thomas (1914-53), Welsh poet.

DYMPHNA—**f** 'One fit to be' (Irish).

EAMON, EAMONN—**m** Irish form of Edmund.

EARL—**m** 'Nobleman' (Old English). Example of a title taken as a forename.

EASTER—**f** Used to christen a child born during this festival, but in earlier days more often found because it was confused with Esther.

EBEN—**m** 'Stone' (Hebrew).

EBENEZER—**m** 'Stone of help' (Hebrew). The name derives from the stone put up by Samuel to commemorate victory over the Philistines: I Samuel 7: 12. Ebenezer Scrooge is the central character in Dickens's *A Christmas Carol* (1843).

EDAN—**m** (Scottish) Variant of Aidan. St Edan was a disciple of St David.

EDELINA—**f** Diminutive of Adela.

EDEN—**m** or **f** 'Delight' (Hebrew). According to the Bible the very first place-name, and therefore a natural, though not widely used, forename. Eden Phillpotts (1862-1960), English novelist.

EDGAR—**m** 'Prosperous spear' (Old English). King of England in 959 though not crowned until 973.

EDITH—**f** 'Rich in battle' (Old English). St Eadgyth (962-84) was the daughter of King Edgar, but in its present form it is a Victorian revival. Edith Cavell (1865-1917), First World War heroine, executed for helping British soldiers to escape.

EDME—**f** Scottish variant of Esme. Its origin is unclear.

EDMOND, EDMUND—**m** 'Wealthy protector' (Old English). St Edmund, king of the East Angles, was martyred by the Danes in 870. Edmund the Magnificent, king of the West Saxons and

Mercians, died 946.

EDNA—**f** 'Rejuvenation' or 'delight' (Hebrew). Could also derive from Old English Edana. Edna Lyall, novelist writing from 1879, may have been the cause of its revival.

EDOM—**m** 'Red' (Hebrew). The byname of Esau, who sold his birthright for a bowl of red lentil soup.

EDRIC—**m** 'Prosperous ruler' (Old English).

EDWARD—**m** 'Wealthy protector' (Old English). Edward the Elder, son of Alfred the Great, ruled the West Saxons 901-24 and set the name of a line of English and British kings down to Edward VIII, who abdicated in 1936.

EDWIN—**m** 'Rich Friend' (Old English). Edwin (died 633), king of Northumbria.

EDWINA—**f** Modern version of Edwin. Edwina Currie (born 1946), Conservative politician.

EDYTHE—**f** Alternative spelling of Edith.

EFFIE—**f** Short for Euphemia. Effie Ruskin, the spurned wife of the writer John Ruskin, later married the painter Millais.

EGAN—**m** English rendering of Gaelic Aogan.

EGBERT—**m** 'Gleaming sword' (Old English). First king of England (died 839).

EGIDIA—**f** Derives from the Latin form of Giles.

EGON—**m** (German). Origin uncertain. There was a St Egon of Augsburg in the twelfth century. Egon Ronay now famous in Britain for his guides to restaurants.

EILEEN—**f** 'Light' (Irish Gaelic). Also a form of Helen.

EILERT—**m** 'Sword hard' (Teutonic). Quite common in Scandinavia.

EINAR—**m** 'Lone Warrior' (Old Norse).

EIRA—**f** 'Snow' (Welsh). Modern invention recalling the weather when the baby was born.

EIREEN—**f** Variant in England and Ireland of Irene.

EIRWEN—**f** 'Pure as the snow' (Welsh). Modern introduction.

EITHNE—**f** Of Irish origin.

ELAINE—**f** A form, in old French, of Helen popularised by Tennyson's account of Lancelot and Elaine.

ELAKSHI—**f** 'Intelligent eyes' (Hindu).

ELDON—**m** Old English place-name derivation.

ELDRED—**m** Form of Aldred.

ELEANOR, ELINOR—**f** A form of Helen, introduced into England by Eleanor of Aquitaine (c.1122—1204), wife of Henry II, but popular through Eleanor (1245-90), queen of Edward I. The beautiful Eleanor crosses were erected to commemorate the journey of her body to burial.

ELEAZAR—**m** 'Helped by God' (Hebrew). The name of Aaron's

eldest surviving son, and his successor as high priest.

ELECTRA—f 'Amber' (Greek). Daughter of Agamemnon who incited her brother Orestes to kill their mother, Clytemnestra.

ELENA—f Italian and Spanish form of Helen.

ELEONORA—f Recent introduction of the old Italian form of Eleanor.

ELFREDA—f 'Elf strength' (Old English), implying supernatural or hidden powers. An Anglo-Saxon name revived in Victorian times. Elfrida was mother of Ethelred the Unready.

ELI—m 'Of the highest' (Hebrew). The high priest who brought up the prophet Samuel. Eli Whitney (1765-1825), American inventor of the cotton-gin.

ELIAS—m Greek form of Elijah. The prophet Elijah is referred to in the New Testament as Elias.

ELIEZER—m Variant of Eleazar.

ELIJAH—m 'Jehovah is God' (Hebrew). Gave rise to surname and, latterly, forename of Ellis.

ELISE, ÉLISE—f German and French forms of Elizabeth.

ELISHA—m 'God's gift' (Hebrew). Prophet who succeeded Elijah.

ELISSA—f Fashionable form of Elizabeth.

ELIZA—f Short form of Elizabeth used by poets in her reign for Queen Elizabeth I (1533-1603). Now used in its own right, e.g. Eliza Doolittle in Shaw's *Pygmalion* (1916).

ELIZABETH, ELISABETH—f 'God is my all' (Hebrew). The mother of St John the Baptist. Spelt with an 's' on the continent. Its popularity directly attributable to Queen Elizabeth I (1533-1603).

ELKANAH—m 'Whom God has created' (Hebrew). Father of the prophet Samuel.

ELLA—f 'All' (Teutonic). Introduced by the Normans and revived in the nineteenth century.

ELLALINE—f Variant of Ella, recorded in 1900.

ELLARD—m 'Nobly endures' (Teutonic).

ELLEN—f Now quite independent form of Helen. Dame Ellen Terry (1848-1928), actress.

ELLERY—m Surname derivation from Latin *hilans*, 'cheerful', or Greek *eulalia*, 'well-spoken'.

ELLIS—m Form of Elijah or Elisha.

ELMA—f An American abbreviation of the Italian female form of William.

ELMER—m Derived from Aylmer and largely confined to the USA.

ELMO—m Corruption of Erasmus, representing, in St Elmo's Castle, a third-century Persian saint. Also popular name of St Peter Gonzalez (died 1246), patron saint of seamen, giving rise to the phenomenon of 'St Elmo's fire' – an electrical discharge from the mast of a ship during a storm.

ELOISA—**f** Anglicised form of Eloise.

ELOISE—**f** (French). From the account of Abélard and Éloïse, star-crossed lovers of the twelfth century.

ELROY—**m** 'The king' (Spanish).

ELSA—**f** From Else, the German short form of Elizabeth; now quite independent.

ELSDON—**m** Place-name in Northumberland, but used largely in the USA.

ELSIE, ELSPETH—**f** Forms of Elizabeth.

ELTON—**m** 'From the old settlement' (Old English).

ELUNED—**f** Welsh form of Lynette.

ELVINA—**f** 'Wise friend' (Teutonic).

ELVIRA—**f** Spanish Visigothic/Teutonic derivation, possible meaning 'wise counsel'. Donna Elvira appears in Mozart's *Don Giovanni* (1787).

ELVIS—**m** 'All wise' (Old Norse). Elvis Aaron Presley (1935-77), American singer, made the name popular.

ELWIN—**m** Form of Alwyn.

EMANUEL—**m** 'God with us' (Hebrew). The name given to Christ as deliverer of Judah, prophesied by Isaiah (7: 14 and 8: 8).

EMERALD—**f** From the green precious stone, a modern innovation.

EMERY—**m** Possibly from Amalric, 'world ruler' (Teutonic).

EMILIA—**f** Variant of Emily, appears as Emulea in 1316. Shakespeare uses it in *A Winter's Tale* for a lady attending Queen Hermione.

EMILY—**f** From the same roots as Amelia and Amalia, perhaps meaning 'worker'. Chaucer wrote of a character called Emelye in his 'Knight's Tale'. Emily Brontë (1818-48), author of *Wuthering Heights*.

EMLYN—**m** 'Hard worker' (Welsh). Of Teutonic origin and still common in Wales. Emlyn Williams (1905-87), Welsh actor and playwright.

EMMA—**f** 'Whole' (Teutonic). Originally a short form of Ermintrude. Emma (died 1052) was the wife of Ethelred the Unready in 1002. Emma Woodhouse, heroine of *Emma* by Jane Austen (1816). Emma, Lady Hamilton (1761-1815), great love of Lord Nelson.

EMMANUEL—**m** Variant of Emanuel.

EMMELINE—**f** Norman variant of Amelia, probably meaning 'worker'. Emmeline Pankhurst (1858-1928), leader of the 'Votes for Women' movement in Britain.

EMRYS—**m** Welsh form of Ambrose.

ENA—**f** 'Little fire' (Irish). Popularised by Princess (Victoria Eugenie Julia) Ena, who became Queen of Spain in 1906.

ENGELBERT—**m** 'Famous Angle' (Teutonic). St Engelbert (1186-1255) was Archbishop of Cologne. Engelbert Humperdinck, popular singer of the 1960s.

ENID—**f** 'Life' (Welsh). Used in England after Tennyson had his 'Geraint and Enid' (part of *Idylls of the King*) published in 1859. Enid Blyton (1897-1968), successful children's author.

ENOCH—**m** 'Experienced' (Hebrew). The father of Methuselah. A book of 'Revelations' is attributed to him. 'Enoch Arden', tragic poem by Tennyson. Enoch Powell, right-wing politician.

ENOLA—**f** Twentieth-century invention of unknown origin. Perhaps intended for an only child, as it spells 'alone' backwards.

ENZO—**m** (Italian) Short form of Lorenzo or Vincenzo.

EPHRAIM—**m** 'Green pastures' (Hebrew). Second son of Joseph, founder of one of the twelve tribes of Israel.

EPHRATA—**f** 'Fruitful' (Hindu).

ERASMUS—**m** 'Beloved' (Greek). Desiderius Erasmus (1465-1536), Dutch scholar of the Renaissance.

ERCOLE—**m** Italian form of Hercules.

ERIC—**m** Nordic name perhaps meaning 'always the ruler' (Teutonic). Twenty Scandinavian kings bore this name. Eric the Red, tenth-century Norse rover, founded Greenland. Revived in the nineteenth century through Dean Farrar's popular school story, *Eric; or, Little by Little* (1858).

ERICA—**f** Form of Eric which first occurred in Edna Lyall's very popular novel *We Two* (1884). Also the Latin name for heather and related plants.

ERIN—**f** 'Peace' (Irish Gaelic). Also a Gaelic name for Ireland and the name of a legendary Irish queen. Especially popular in Ireland and the USA.

ERITH—**f** One mention only found. Derived from the owner's birthplace in Kent, the name of which means 'gravel harbour'.

ERMINE—**f** From the fur, but could be variant of Hermione.

ERMINTRUDE—**f** 'All powerful' or 'wholly beloved' (Teutonic). A Victorian fashion that has died away.

ERNEST—**m** 'Earnestness' (German). Introduced by the Hanoverians and revived by the Victorians, perhaps through Queen Victoria's uncle, Ernest I of Saxe-Coburg-Gotha (1771-1851). Further publicised by Oscar Wilde's play *The Importance of Being Earnest* (1893).

ERNESTINE—**f** Form of Ernest.

ERROL—**f** A variant of Earl. May also derive from the Scottish place-name and the Earls of Erroll. Errol Flynn (1909-59),

American film actor.

ERSKINE—**m** Surname or place-name derivation. Influenced by Erskine Childers (1870-1922), author of *Riddle of the Sands*, spy thriller.

ERWIN—**m** 'Honourable friend' (Teutonic). Very old German forename, revived through Erwin Rommel (1891-1944), German field marshal in the Second World War.

ESAU—**m** 'Blind' (Hebrew). The elder son of Isaac and twin brother of Jacob, to whom he sold his birthright for a bowl of red lentil soup.

ESDRAS—**m** 'Help' (Hebrew).

ESMÉ—**m** or **f** 'Beloved' (Old French). Came to England from France via Scotland.

ESMERALDA—**f** 'Emerald' (Spanish). Character in Victor Hugo's *Notre Dame de Paris*.

ESMOND—**m** 'Gracious protection' (Old English).

ESPERANCE—**f** 'Hope' (French).

ESTELLE—**f** 'Star' (French). The heroine of Dickens's *Great Expectations* (1860).

ESTHER—**f** 'Myrtle' (Persian). One of the books of the Old Testament. Oratorio by Handel based on Racine's play *Esther*.

ESWEN—**f** 'Strength' (Welsh).

ETHAN—**m** 'Never-failing [stream]' (Hebrew). The title of Psalm 89. Ethan Allen (1738-89), American revolutionary figure, made it popular in the USA.

ETHEL—**f** 'Noble' (Old English). A component of Saxon names which finally became used separately.

ETHELDRED, ETHELDREDA—**f** 'Noble strength' (Old English). St Etheldreda (died 769) was queen of Northumbria, founder of a convent at Ely, where the cathedral was built over her remains. This name is related to Audrey.

ETHELINDA—**f** 'Noble serpent' (Teutonic).

ETHELRED—**m** 'Noble counsel' (Old English). King of Wessex (866-71) and brother of Alfred. Ethelred, son of Edgar, was king of England 978-1016 and was called the *Unread* ('uncounselled'), a pun on his name that later developed into 'the Unready'.

ETTA—**f** Short form of several names like Margaretta and Violetta.

EUAN—**m** Anglicised form of Ewen.

EUDO—**m** Tentatively linked with *jôdh,* 'child' (Old Norse). Introduced by the Normans.

EUDORA—**f** A made-up name possibly reflecting a meaning of 'well-given' or 'good gift'. Eudora Welty (born 1909), American writer.

EUGENE—**m** 'Well-born' (Greek). A line of popes from the seventh century. Made popular by the exploits of Prince Eugene of Savoy (1663-1736), the military strategist. *Eugene Onegin*, opera by Tchaikovsky.

EUGENIE, EUGENIA—**f** Form of Eugene. Empress Eugénie (1826-1920) of France, wife of Napoleon III. Princess Eugenie (born 1990), daughter of Prince Andrew.

EULALIA—**f** 'Well-spoken' (Greek).

EUNICE—**f** 'Good victory' (Greek). Could also relate to the Greek *euris,* 'wife'. The mother of Timothy (II Timothy 1: 5).

EUPHEMIA—**f** 'Fair speech' (Greek). A virgin-martyr of Bithynia.

EUPHROSYNE—**f** 'Cheerfulness' (Greek). One of the Three Graces.

EURWYN—**m** 'Golden' (Welsh).

EUSEBIO—**m** 'I am pious' (Greek). Many early saints so named.

EUSTACE—**m** 'Fruitful' (Greek). Patron saint of huntsmen.

EUSTACIA—**f** Form of Eustace.

EVADNE—**f** Greek name of uncertain meaning. In Greek mythology Evadne was a self-sacrificing wife.

EVAN—**m** Welsh form of John.

EVANDER—**m** 'Good man' (Greek).

EVANGELINE—**f** 'Bringer of good news' (Greek). Invention attributed to Henry Longfellow for the heroine of his poem 'Evangeline' (1847).

EVE, EVA—**f** 'Lively' (Hebrew). In the Bible, the first woman, the mother of the human race. Little Eva in *Uncle Tom's Cabin* (1852) by Harriet Beecher Stowe had considerable influence on its use.

EVELINA—**f** A variant of Eve or Evelyn. Revived by Fanny Burney for her novel of that name in 1778.

EVELYN—**m** or **f** Derives from a surname based on the Norman female name Aveline. Evelyn Waugh (1898-1981), English novelist.

EVERARD—**m** 'Tough as a boar' (Teutonic). Everard Webley, character in Huxley's *Point Counter Point* (1928).

EVERIL—**f** Form of Averil.

EVITA—**f** (Spanish). Diminutive of Eva. Eva Duarte de Perón (1919-52) was called this by adoring Argentinians.

EWEN, EWAN—**m** 'Well-born' (Celtic). Though more in favour in Scotland, it was once common in England too.

EZEKIEL—**m** 'May God strengthen' (Hebrew). Hebrew prophet.

EZRA—**m** 'Help' (Hebrew). Hebrew scribe and priest, author of one of the books of the Old Testament. Ezra Pound (1885-1972), American poet.

FABIAN—**m** Roman family name of which the original meaning is obscure. Third-century pope and martyr. The Fabian Society is a left-wing intellectual organisation.

FABIO—**m** Italian, derived from the old Roman family Fabius.

FABIOLA—**f** Diminutive form of Fabian.

FABRON—**m** 'The little blacksmith' (French). Also spelt as Faber.

FADILLA—**f** (French) Diminutive of Françoise, i.e. Frances.

FADOUL—**m** 'Honest' (Arabic).

FAIDA—**f** 'Abundant' (Arabic).

FAINE—**f** 'Joyful' (Old English).

FAIRFAX—**m** 'Fair-haired' (Anglo-Saxon).

FAISAL—**m** 'Wise judge' (Arabic).

FAITH—**f** A 'virtue' name. Not used until after the Reformation and now less popular.

FALAH—**m** 'Success' (Arabic).

FALK—**m** 'Falcon' (Hebrew).

FANNY—**f** Short form of Frances.

FARIDA—**f** 'Precious gem' (Arabic).

FARLEY—**m** 'Further meadow' (Old English). Surname/place-name derivation.

FATIMA—**f** Mohammed's daughter. Roman Catholics adopted it after the vision in Portugal in 1917 of Our Lady of Fatima.

FAVIAN—**m** 'A man of understanding' (Latin).

FAWAZ—**m** 'Victorious' (Arabic).

FAY—**f** 'Fairy'. May have started out as a pet-name for Faith.

FAYAD—**m** 'Generous' (Arabic).

FELICIA—**f** A variant of Felicity.

FELICITY—**f** 'Happiness' (Latin). One of the many abstract names which became popular from the seventeenth century.

FELIX—**m** 'Happy' (Latin). St Felix, an East Anglian saint, gave Felixstowe, Suffolk, its name. There are over fifty saints who bear this name. Sir Felix Aylmer (1889-1979), English actor.

FENELLA—**f** Anglicised form of Fiennuala, 'white shoulder' (Irish Gaelic). Character in Scott's *Peveril of the Peak*. Fenella Fielding, actress.

FERDINAND—**m** 'Venturesome' (Teutonic). Borne by many kings of Castile. Ferdinand de Lesseps (1805-94), architect of the Suez Canal.

FERGAL—**m** 'Man of valour' (Irish). Anglicised spelling of Fearghal.

FERGUS—**m** 'The chosen man' (Old Irish). Fergus I was in legend the first Irish king of Scotland, some time in the sixth century.

FERIDE—**m** 'Unique' (Turkish).

FERN—**f** Plant name.

FIDEL—**m** 'Faithful' (Latin). Fidel Castro (born 1927), president of Cuba.

FIFI—**f** Diminutive of Josephine.

FINBAR—**m** 'Fair-haired' (Irish Gaelic). Anglicised form of Fionnbarr, sixth-century bishop of Cork, later beatified.

FINLAY—**m** 'Fair warrior' (Gaelic).

FIONA—**f** 'Fair' (Gaelic). Tentative derivation of name probably invented by William Sharp (1855-1905) for his character 'Fiona Macleod'.

FIORELLA—**f** 'Little flower' (Italian).

FIRMIN—**m** 'Steadfast' (French). Name of several early Christian saints.

FLAXIA—**f** 'Flaxen-haired' (Latin).

FLETCHER—**m** 'Arrow-maker' (French). A derivation from the surname. Fletcher Christian was the ringleader of the *Bounty* mutiny (1789).

FLEUR—**f** 'Flower' (French). A character in John Galsworthy's *The Forsyte Saga* (1906-22).

FLICK—**f** Diminutive of Felicity.

FLOELLA—**f** An American invention combining Flora or Florence and Ella. Floella Benjamin, television presenter.

FLORA—**f** The Roman Goddess of flowers, called Chloris by the Greeks. St Flora was martyred in Spain in 850. Flora Macdonald (1722-90), Scottish Jacobite heroine, made the name popular in that country.

FLORENCE—**m** or **f** 'Blooming' (Latin). Usually a girl's name. Florence Nightingale (1820-1912), who was named after the Italian city in which she was born, made it popular.

FLORETTA—**f** 'Little flower' (Latin).

FLORIAN—**m** Used in 1997. From Latin for 'flowery'. Name of a fourth-century saint of fire and drought. More commonly used in the middle ages.

FLOWER—**f** A modern version of Florence.

FLOYD—**m** English adaptation of the Welsh Lloyd.

FONDA—**f** 'Affectionate' (English). A modern rendering of 'fonder'.

FORBES—**m** Derivation from the Scottish surname gained from the Gaelic meaning 'district' or 'fields', as applied to lands in Aberdeenshire. Sir Johnston Forbes-Robertson (1853-1937) and his daughter Jean (1905-62) were well-known actor-managers.

FORD—**m** River and place-name derivation influenced by Henry

Ford (1863-1947), the famous car manufacturer.

FRANCES, FRANCESCA—**f** 'Frenchwoman' (Italian). Form of Francis. Madame D'Arblay (1752-1840) is better known as Frances (Fanny) Burney, author of several famous novels.

FRANCINE—**f** Anglicised version of Françoise, French feminine of Francis.

FRANCIS—**m** 'Frenchman' or 'Frank' (Latin) from Old German *franc* ('free'). Further derived from the fact that even under the Romans there were men who considered themselves 'franks' or free men. Rulers of France, Austria and Sicily have been thus named. St Francis of Assisi (1182-1226) was founder of the order of Franciscans.

FRANÇOISE—**f** French form of Frances.

FRANK—**m** Short form of Francis but now used in its own right.

FRANKLIN—**m** 'Freeman' (Old English). Popular in the USA through Benjamin Franklin (1706-90), statesman and scientist, and Franklin D. Roosevelt (1882-1945), president during the Second World War.

FRASER—**m** From the Scottish surname.

FREDA—**f** 'Peace' (Old English). Also a short form of Winifred.

FREDERIC, FREDERICK—**m** 'Peaceful ruler' (Teutonic). Frederick the Great (1712-86) created the state of Prussia.

FREDERICA—**f** Victorian female form of Frederick.

FREYA—**f** From the Nordic goddess Freyja. Dame Freya Stark (1893-1993), English travel writer.

FRUSANNAH—**f** Artificial combination of Frances and Susannah; pet form is Frusie.

FULBERT—**m** 'Very bright' (Teutonic).

FULK, FULKE—**m** 'People' (Teutonic). Originally a short form of compound names. Sir Fulke Greville (1554-1628), English poet and statesman.

FULVIA—**f** 'Tawny-coloured' [hair] (Latin).

GABRIEL—**m** 'Strong man of God' (Hebrew). The archangel who announced to Zachariah the birth of his son, John the Baptist, and to the Virgin Mary the birth of Jesus Christ. Gabriel Fahrenheit (1686-1736) introduced the mercury thermometer.

GABRIELLE—**f** Form of Gabriel from France.

GABY, GABI—**f** (French). Affectionate form of Gabrielle.

GAIL—**f** Short form of Abigail.

GALE—**f** A shortened form of Abigail.

GALEN—**m** 'Calm' (Greek). Claudius Galenus was a Graeco-Roman writer on medicine in the second century AD.

GALFRIDA—**f** Form of Geoffrey.

GALIA—**f** 'God has redeemed' (Hebrew).

GAMALAT—**m** 'Beautiful one' (Arabic).

GAMALIEL—**m** 'God's reward' (Hebrew). Underlining the value of a male child in early communities.

GAMMA—**f** The third letter of the Greek alphabet (equivalent to G), sometimes used to name a third child.

GANESH—**m** 'King of the crowd' (Hindu). Hindu god of wisdom with the head of an elephant and the body of a man.

GARDENIA—**f** Flower name of recent introduction.

GARETH—**m** Arose from a mistake by Malory in transcribing a Welsh name for a character in his *Morte d'Arthur* (1469-70) and repeated by Tennyson in his *Gareth and Lynnet*, which made it popular.

GARFIELD—**m** Surname derivation, but may have been made more popular through the comic-strip cat of the 1980s. Sir Garfield Sobers, West Indian cricketer (born 1936).

GARLAND—**f** 'Crown of blossoms' (French).

GARNET—**m** or **f** From the precious stone. Garnet Joseph, Viscount Wolseley (1833-1913), British general, gave rise to the saying, 'All Sir Garnet …'.

GARRETT—**m** From the medieval dialect pronunciation of Gerard. Found in Camden's list of 'usual Christian names' of 1605. Now used mostly in Ireland.

GARTH—**m** 'Garden' (Old Norse). Surname from a worker in a garden. Used as a forename in books by nineteenth-century authors like Wilkie Collins and Charlotte M. Yonge. Garth Crooks was a famous footballer of the 1980s.

GARY—**m** Short form of Gareth, Garrett, Garth and possibly Gerard. Gary Cooper (1901-61), film actor.

GASPAR—**m** 'Master of the treasure' (Persian).

GASTON—**m** 'Man of Gascony' (French). Common French name which has some currency in Britain.

GAVIN—**m** Celtic name of uncertain origin, appearing in early French stories as Gauvain and as Gawain in the legend of King Arthur.

GAY—**f** 'Happy' or 'merry'. An example of the vogue for naming girls after abstract qualities.

GAYLORD—**m** 'Jolly' (Old French).

GAYNOR—**f** Phonetic form of Welsh Gwenhwyfar, otherwise Guinevere.

GEMMA—**f** 'Precious stone' (Italian).

GENE—**m** Short form of Eugene. Gene Kelly (born 1912), dancer and actor.

GENESIA—**f** 'Newcomer' (Latin).

GENETTE—**f** Variant of Jeanette.

GENEVA—**f** Influenced by the French Geneviève more than by the Swiss city.

GENEVIEVE—**f** 'White wave' (Celtic). St Geneviève of Brabant was the eighth-century heroine of later legends. Heroine of Coleridge's poem 'Love'. Title of a film about a veteran car which, strangely, may account for a modest revival.

GENEVRA—**f** Origin uncertain. Genevra Caws QC, died 1997.

GENISTA—**f** Flower name from the Latin for 'broom'.

GEOFFREY—**m** 'Pledge of peace' or 'peaceful land' (Teutonic). Geoffrey Chaucer (c.1345-1400), famed for his *Canterbury Tales*.

GEORGE—**m** 'Tiller of the soil' (Greek). St George, patron saint of England, was a Roman military tribune martyred in 303. His dragon-killing was legendary. The house of Hanover gave Britain royal Georges for 116 years and brought the name thoroughly into favour.

GEORGIANA, GEORGINA—**f** Forms of George. Lady Georgiana Spencer (born 1757) was a beauty painted by both Reynolds and Gainsborough and an ancestor of Lady Diana Spencer.

GERAINT—**m** Welsh name, perhaps ultimately from the Greek for 'old man'. Geraint was one of Arthur's knights.

GERALD—**m** 'Spear power' (Teutonic).

GERALDINE—**f** Form of Gerald said to have been invented by Henry Howard, Earl of Surrey, about 1540 in his poems concerning Lady Elizabeth Fitzgerald.

GERARD—**m** 'Spear-sharp' (Teutonic). Gerard the Blessed founded the Order of Hospitallers of St John of Jerusalem in 1080. Gerard Manley Hopkins (1844-89), English poet.

GERBOLD—**m** 'Bold spear' (Teutonic).

GERDA—**f** A giant maiden in Norse mythology, wife of Freyr, who became an emblem of peace and blessing (Old Norse). The name was popularised by Hans Christian Andersen (1805-75), who used it in *The Snow Queen*.

GERMAIN, GERMAINE—**f** 'Of Germany' (Latin). Germaine Greer (born 1939), Australian writer on feminist issues.

GERTRUDE—**f** 'Spear-strong' (Teutonic). The seventh-century saint Gertrude of Nivelles became a patron saint of travellers. Gertrude, queen of Denmark and mother of Hamlet in Shakespeare's play.

GERVAIS, GERVASE—**m** Unknown derivation. Its use stems from St Gervasius. Gervase of Canterbury and Gervase of Tilbury were medieval English chroniclers.

GERWYN—**m** 'Fair love' (Welsh).

GETHIN—**m** 'Dark-skinned' (Welsh).

GHISLAIN, GHISLAINE—**f** Origin unclear, could be a form of Giselle. Used in Britain from the end of the Second World War. Robert Maxwell (1923-91) named his yacht *Lady Ghislaine* after his daughter.

GIDEON—**m** 'Having only a stump for a hand' (Hebrew). Hebrew religious reformer.

GIGI—**f** Pet-name for Gilberte, the French feminine of Gilbert. Used by Colette in her novel *Gigi* (1945) and popularised by the musical based on it in 1958.

GILBERT—**m** 'Honour bright' (Teutonic). St Gilbert (thirteenth century) was the last Scotsman to be canonised.

GILBY—**m** 'The pledge', 'a hostage'. Also spelt Gilbey.

GILDA—**f** Italian, from a Teutonic word meaning 'sacrifice'. The heroine in Verdi's opera *Rigoletto* (1851).

GILES, GYLES—**m** Ultimately derived from Greek *aigidion,* 'kid'. Possibly meant 'wearer of a goat-skin'. Gyles Brandreth (born 1948), author and television personality.

GILLIAN—**f** Popular English form of Julian. As Gillot it was once used to describe a flirt and so 'to jilt'.

GILMOUR—**m** 'Servant of Mary [mother of Jesus]' (Gaelic). Developed from the surname.

GINA—**f** Short form of Georgina.

GINETTE—**f** French; pet form of Geneviève.

GINNY—**f** Pet form of Virginia.

GISELA, GISELLE—**f** 'Honourable' (Teutonic).

GITA—**f** 'Song' (Hindi).

GITIKA—**f** 'Little song' (Hindu).

GLADWIN—**m** 'Kind friend' (Anglo-Saxon).

GLADYS—**f** (Welsh) Appears from time immemorial as the Welsh version (Gwladys) of the Latin Claudia. Its revival in England is only from the nineteenth century.

GLEN, GLENN—**m** 'Valley' (Celtic). Sometimes feminine as in Glenn Close (born 1947), American actress.

GLENCORA—**f** One of the strongest characters in the political novels of Anthony Trollope (1815-82).

GLENDA—**f** 'Good' (Welsh). Glenda Jackson (born 1936), English actress and politician.

GLENYS—**f** Modern made-up name, perhaps meaning 'pure'.

GLORIA—**f** 'Glory' (Latin). Of late Victorian origin.

GLYNIS—**f** 'Little valley' (Welsh).

GODDARD—**m** 'Strong through God' (Old English).

GODFREY—**m** 'Peace of God' (Teutonic).

GODIVA—**f** 'God's gift' (Old English). Heroine (died 1080) who rode naked through Coventry, to protest at injustice.

GODRIC—**m** 'Ruling through God' (Old English). Eleventh-century English saint and hermit.

GODWIN—**m** 'God's champion' (Old English). Godwin(e), Earl of the West Saxons, who died in 1053, was father of King Harold.

GOLDWIN—**m** 'Valued friend' or 'good friend' (Old English).

GOODWIN—**m** 'Good friend' (Old English). Modern use of an old surname.

GORDON—**m** Originally from the Scottish family name, but its use as a forename received impetus from the career of General Gordon (1833-85).

GORONWY—**m** 'Hero' (Welsh). A character in the *Mabinogion*.

GRACE—**f** One of the 'virtue' names.

GRACILIA—**f** 'Slender' (Latin).

GRAEME—**m** Scottish form of Graham.

GRAHAM—**m** Very popular recent adoption of an old Scottish family name. Graham Greene (1904-91), English novelist.

GRANT—**m** 'Great' or 'big' (Old French).

GRANVILLE—**m** From the surname of a Norman baron.

GREGORY—**m** 'Watchful' (Greek). Two early fathers of the Eastern church and a line of sixteen popes from St Gregory the Great (*c*.540-604).

GRENVILLE—**m** French family name from which came the great English family of statesmen.

GRETA—**f** A Swedish pet form of Margaret. Greta Garbo (1905-90), Swedish-born film actress.

GRIFFIN, GRIFFITH—**m** Welsh name containing the element *udd*, 'lord'. Borne by several Welsh princes.

GRIMBALD—**m** 'Fierce and bold' (Old English). A monk of St Omer, established in Oxford by King Alfred to promote learning there, became an Anglo-Saxon saint (died 903).

GRISELDA—**f** 'Grey battle' or possibly 'fight for Christ' (Teutonic). Chaucer told Griselda's story in his 'Clerk's Tale'.

GRISWOLD—**m** Surname/place-name derivation, meaning 'grey moor' (Old English).

GUINEVERE—**f** 'White and smooth' (Welsh). Form of the Welsh Gwenhwyfar, queen of King Arthur.

GULSHAN—**m** 'Garden' (Muslim). Strangely popular.

GUNTER—**m** 'War-hard' (Teutonic). Günter Grass (born 1927),

German author.

GUSTAV, GUSTAVUS—**m** Uncertain Nordic derivation, perhaps meaning 'staff of the gods'. Made popular through a line of Swedish kings from 1523. Gustav Holst (1874-1934), English composer.

GUY—**m** 'Broad' (Teutonic). A Norman introduction. Latinised as Guido. The notorious Guy Fawkes (1570-1606) caused a hiatus in its use until modern times. Thomas Guy, bookseller, founded Guy's Hospital in 1722.

GWENDA—**f** A modern invention meaning 'fair and good' (Welsh).

GWENDOLEN, GWENDOLINE—**f** 'White-browed' (Welsh). Appears in Arthurian legend.

GWYNETH, GWYNNETH—**f** 'Bliss' (Welsh).

GWYNFOR—**m** 'Fair place' (Welsh).

HABACUC—**m** 'Embrace' (Hebrew). One of the prophets' books of the Bible (Habakkuk).

HABEEB, HABIB—**m** 'Beloved' (Muslim).

HACON—**m** 'Right-hand man' (Old Norse). As Haakon, represents a line of kings of Norway stretching back to 934.

HADAR—**m** 'Ornament' (Hebrew).

HADDON—**m** 'Heather hill' (Old English). Place-name/surname derivation.

HADWIN—**m** 'Friend of the same rank' (Old English).

HADYN—**m** A twentieth-century variant of Haydn used mostly in Wales.

HAFIZ—**m** 'He who remembers' (Arabic).

HAGAR—**f** 'Forsaken' (Hebrew).

HAIDAR—**m** 'Lion' (Arabic).

HAIDEE—**f** Invented by Byron for a character in his poem 'Don Juan' (1824), possibly from the Greek for 'modest'.

HAL—**m** Form of Henry.

HALE—**m** Place-name/surname derivation.

HALEY—**f** Variant of Hayley.

HALINA—**f** A Polish name, from the Greek for 'sun'.

HAM—**m** Relates to the Hebrew word for 'hot', implying 'From the hot lands' (the progenitor of the Hamites who lived in the south). Ham was the son of Noah.

HAMAL—**m** 'The lamb' (Arabic).

HAMILTON—**m** Scottish place-name.

HAMISH—**m** Gaelic form of James, said to have been popularised by William Black (1841-98), who often used the name for characters in his novels.

HAMLET—**m** Shakespeare's Hamlet derives his name from the Nordic Amlóthi. Otherwise, Hamlet is a derivative of Hamon.

HAMNET—**m** Diminutive of Hamon. Shakespeare gave the name to his son, twin of Judith, in 1585.

HAMON—**m** Norman introduction, from the Teutonic word for 'home'.

HANIF, HANEEF—**m** 'Guided rightly' (Muslim). Hanif Mohammad, member of Pakistan cricket team, famous in the 1950s.

HANK—**m** Pet form of Henry, largely confined to USA.

HANNAH—**f** 'God has favoured me' (Hebrew). The mother of the prophet Samuel.

HANNIBAL—**m** 'The grace of Baal' (Phoenician). Hannibal (died c.183 BC) was a great Carthaginian general. The name was at one time a favourite in Cornwall, perhaps because of the trade in tin with the Phoenicians.

HANS—**m** (German, Dutch, Danish) Form of John. Hans Christian Andersen (1805-75), Danish storyteller.

HANSIKA—**f** 'Beautiful little swan' (Hindu).

HAPPY—**m** or **f** Foretelling how, it is hoped, the baby's character will develop.

HARCOURT—**m** French place-name.

HARDY—**m** Surname derivation. Thomas Hardy (1840-1928), English novelist and poet. Sir Thomas Masterman Hardy served with Nelson on the *Victory* at the battle of Trafalgar (1805).

HARI—**m** Several meanings, more importantly as another name for the gods Vishnu, Shiva and Shira.

HARIKA—**f** 'Most beautiful' (Turkish).

HARMONIA—**f** 'Unifying' (Greek).

HAROLD—**m** 'Leader of men' (Old English). Harold Godwinson lost the throne of England to William the Conqueror in 1066.

HARPER—**m** or **f** Surname meaning 'a player of the harp'.

HARRIET—**f** Form of Harry and so deriving from Henry. Often abbreviated to Hattie. Harriet Beecher Stowe (1811-96) wrote *Uncle Tom's Cabin* (1851).

HARRIS—**m** 'Son of Harry' (English). Use as a forename peaked at the beginning of the twentieth century, now rare.

HARRISON—**m** Obvious surname derivation, perhaps influenced by Harrison Ford (born 1942), American actor.

HARRY—**m** Affectionate form of Henry now used independently.

Harry S. Truman (1884-1972), thirty-third President of the USA.

HARSHIDA—**f** 'Giver of joy' (Hindu).

HARTLEY—**m** Place-name/surname derivation. Sir Hartley Shawcross was the British prosecutor at the Nuremberg Trials of Nazi leaders.

HARTWIN—**m** 'Brave friend' (Teutonic).

HARVEY—**m** 'Battle-worthy' (Old Breton).

HASAN, HASSAN—**m** 'Handsome, good-looking' (Muslim).

HASNA—**f** 'Beautiful' (Turkish).

HATTIE—**f** Affectionate form of Harriet now used independently.

HAVELOCK—**m** 'Sea-port' (Old Norse). Place-name/surname derivation.

HAWIS—**f** 'Worth fighting for' (Teutonic). Common enough in the twelfth century to give rise to the surname Hawes.

HAYA—**f** 'Life' (Hebrew).

HAYDN, HAYDEN, HAYDON—**m** Probably a Welsh variant of Aidan but may also be a conscious reference to the composer.

HAYLEY—**f** Surname origin. Hayley Mills, actress.

HAZAR—**f** 'Nightingale' (Arabic).

HAZEL—**m** or **f** One of the Victorian plant names.

HEATHCLIFF—**m** Hero of Emily Brontë's *Wuthering Heights* (1847).

HEATHER—**f** Plant name of Victorian vintage.

HEBE—**f** 'Young' (Greek). Greek goddess of youth and cup-bearer to the gods.

HECTOR—**m** 'One who restrains' (Greek). Son of Priam, and defender of Troy, killed by Achilles.

HEDDA—**f** 'Strife battle' (Teutonic). *Hedda Gabler* (1890), play by the Norwegian dramatist Henrik Ibsen.

HEDLEY—**m** 'Heather-girt clearing' (Old English). Place-name/surname derivation. Use began in Victorian times.

HEDY—**f** Short form of German Hedwig ('strife battle'), now used separately. Inspired by Austrian film actress Hedy Lamarr (Hedwig Kiesler) before the Second World War.

HEIDI—**f** Diminutive of Adelheid. Title of a children's book by Johanna Spyri (1881), which gave currency to the name.

HELEN, HELENA—**f** 'Sunbeam' (Greek). Helen of Troy, wife of Menelaus, King of Sparta. St Helena (died 338) was the reputed daughter of Cunobelin (Old King Cole) and mother of the Emperor Constantine.

HELGA—**f** 'Holy' (Old Norse).

HELIANTHE—**f** 'Sunflower' (Greek).

HENGIST—**m** 'Like a stallion' (Teutonic). Jutish invader of Britain (449) with his brother Horsa.

HENRIETTA—**f** Form of Henry brought to England by Henrietta Maria, wife of Charles I.

HENRY—**m** 'Head of the house' (Teutonic). Henry I (1068-1135), William the Conqueror's youngest son, and a long line of English kings down to Henry VIII.

HEPHZIBAH—**f** 'My delight is in her' (Hebrew). The wife of Hezekiah, king of Judah about 700 BC. Hephzibah Menuhin (1920-81), pianist and sister of violinist Yehudi.

HEPSEY—**f** Diminutive of Hephzibah now used in its own right.

HERA—**f** Greek goddess, wife of Zeus

HERBERT—**m** 'Famous army' (Teutonic). Early name that fell into neglect until about 1900, when its revival may have been a compliment to the noble family of that name.

HERCULES—**m** 'Noble fame' (Greek). Original meaning is tentative. Name of the son of Zeus, and of a constellation. Hercule Poirot, Belgian detective character in crime stories by Agatha Christie.

HEREWARD—**m** 'Protector of the army' (Old English). Hereward the Wake, Saxon rebel against William the Conqueror, subject of the novel of the same name by Charles Kingsley (1866).

HERMAN—**m** 'Soldier' (Teutonic). Not so popular since the Second World War when it was associated with Hermann Göring.

HERMIA—**f** Derived from Hermes, messenger to the Greek gods, and popularised by the character in Shakespeare's *A Midsummer Night's Dream*.

HERMIONE—**f** Form of Hermes. In ancient legend, wife of Cadmus, founder of Thebes. Used by Shakespeare for his queen in *A Winter's Tale*.

HERO—**f** Probably from the goddess Hera. The great love of Leander in the classical legend. English use dates from its appearance in Shakespeare's *Much Ado About Nothing*.

HESKETH—**m** Place-name/surname meaning 'race course'.

HESTER—**f** Latin version of Esther.

HETTIE—**f** An affectionate form of Hester now used independently.

HEULWEN—**f** 'Sunshine' (Welsh). Used in Wales since about 1930.

HEZEKIAH—**m** 'God is my strength' (Hebrew). King of Judah, *c*. 700 BC.

HIBERNIA—**f** 'Ireland' (Latin).

HILARY—**m** or **f** 'Cheerful' (Latin). St Hilarius of Poitiers died 368. Hilaire Belloc (1870-1953), author, shows French form.

HILDA—**f** Short form of names beginning with the element *hild,* 'battle' (Teutonic). St Hilda (614-80) founded Whitby Abbey in

657. Name revived in the nineteenth century.

HILDEBRAND—**m** 'Flaming battle sword' (Teutonic). St Hildebrand (1000-85) was Pope Gregory VII.

HILDEGARD, HILDEGARDE—**f** 'War stronghold' (Teutonic). St Hildegard, abbess and founder of the convent of Rupertsberg in 1148.

HILMA—**f** Short form of Wilhelmina, first recorded in Sweden in the nineteeth century. Used as an independent name in Britain since about 1920.

HIMMET—**m** 'Helpful, supportive' (Turkish).

HIPPOLYTA—**f** Form of Hippolytus. Name of the queen of the Amazons, as shown in *A Midsummer Night's Dream*.

HIPPOLYTUS—**m** 'Letting horses loose' (Greek). Son of Theseus and Hippolyta, queen of the Amazons. St Hippolytus, a Roman martyred in 252.

HIRAM—**m** 'Brother of the exalted' (Hebrew). Short for Ahiram, name of a king of Tyre in Old Testament times.

HOLDEN—**m** Place-name/surname meaning 'hollow valley'. Holden Caulfield is the central character in *The Catcher in the Rye* (1951) by J. D. Salinger.

HOLLY—**f** Plant name, especially for Christmas children.

HOMER—**m** Poet (before 700 BC) who wrote the *Iliad* and the *Odyssey*.

HONEY—**f** From the term of sweet endearment.

HONEYSUCKLE—**f** Inferring the sweetness of the flower.

HONOR, HONORIA—**f** 'Of good repute' (Latin).

HONOUR—**f** One of the abstract quality names popular after the Reformation.

HOPE—**f** Abstract quality name, of obvious derivation.

HOPKIN—**m** A pet form of Robert or Robin more popular in the nineteenth century.

HORACE, HORATIO—**m** Roman family name. Horatius Cocles defended the bridge over the Tiber against the invading Etruscans. Quintus Horatius Flaccus ('Horace') became one of the great Latin poets. Horatio, first Viscount Nelson (1758-1805), beat the French at Trafalgar.

HORATIA—**f** Form of Horatio given by Nelson to his daughter by Emma, Lady Hamilton.

HORTENSIA—**f** Form of Hortensius.

HORTENSIUS—**m** 'Gardener' (Latin). A Roman family name.

HOSANNA—**m** or **f** 'Save now' (Hebrew). The crowd's cry to Jesus on his last entry into Jerusalem.

HOWARD—**m** (Teutonic). Uncertain derivation but its most appealing interpretation is 'guardian of my heart. English use derived much later from the great family surname.

HOWELL—**m** Anglicised form of Hywel, meaning 'eminent'.

HUBERT—**m** 'Joyous spirit' (Teutonic). St Hubert (656-727), Bishop of Liège, is patron saint of huntsmen.

HUGH—**m** 'Great-hearted' (Teutonic). Latinised as Hugo. St Hugh of Lincoln (*c*.1135-1200), Bishop of Lincoln.

HUGO—**m** Latinised form of Hugh.

HUMBERT—**m** 'Famous giant' (Teutonic).

HUMPHREY—**m** 'Peaceful giant' (Teutonic).

HUNTER—**m** An occupational surname derivation.

HUW—**m** (Welsh). A variant of Hugh now used far beyond Wales.

HYACINTH—**m** or **f** A Greek word meaning a purple flower or a blue gem (sapphire). Most commonly female.

HYMAN—**m** 'Life' (Hebrew). Equivalent of the feminine Eve. Brought to notice by the humorous book *The Education of Hyman Caplan* by Leonard Q. Ross.

HYPATIA—**f** 'Highest' (Greek). Implying greatest joy at her birth.

HYWEL—**m** 'Eminent' (Welsh).

IAN, IAIN—**m** Scottish form of John.

IANTHE—**f** 'Violet flower' (Greek). Ianthe Eliza was the daughter of the poet Shelley and Harriet Westbrook.

IBRAHIM—**m** Variant of Abraham.

IDA—**f** 'Worker' (Teutonic). Its revival has been attributed to its use by Tennyson for *The Princess* (1847), which was used as the basis for Gilbert and Sullivan's *Princess Ida* (1884).

IDRIS—**m** 'Fiery lord' (Welsh). Cader Idris, the mountain, was so named as the legendary home of Idris the Giant, a mythical magician in Celtic lore. Idris I, first king (from 1951) of the united kingdom of Libya.

IDWAL—**m** 'Within the lord's walls' (Welsh). Place-name/surname origin. A thousand years old and still occasionally used.

IFOR—**m** (Welsh). Derivation uncertain. Not to be confused with Ivor.

IGNATIA—**f** 'Fiery one' (Latin). Ignatius Loyola (1491-1556) was a Spanish soldier who founded the Society of Jesus (Jesuits).

IGOR—**m** Russian form of Inguar ('Ing's warrior'; Old Norse). Prince Igor (1150-1202), great Russian hero.

IKE—**m** Affectionate form of Isaac used independently. It was the nickname of Dwight D. Eisenhower (1890-1969), thirty-fourth President of the USA.

ILANA—**f** 'Tree' (Hebrew). A modern Jewish name.

ILEEN, ILEENE—**f** Variant spellings of Eileen.

ILMA—**f** Affectionate short form of Wilma, itself derived from Wilhelmina.

ILONA—**f** (Hungarian). Form of Helen used in English from at least 1939. Ilona Massey, actress appearing in films from 1937, may have started the fashion.

ILSA—**f** Form of Elizabeth.

IMELDA—**f** (Italian). Italian form of old German implying 'warrior in battle'. Fourteenth-century saint Imelda Lambertini. Imelda Marcos, widow of former president of the Philippines. English spelling is Imalda.

IMMANUEL—**m** Another spelling of Emanuel.

IMOGEN—**f** Heroine of Shakespeare's *Cymbeline*. He probably intended to write Innogen as in Holinshed's *Chronicles*, the source of his inspiration. Walter de la Mare wrote the poem 'To Imogen'.

INA—**f** Affectionate shortening of many names ending in this way from Christina to Wilhelmina, and now used independently.

INDIA—**f** Introduced by Margaret Mitchell in *Gone with the Wind*, filmed in 1939. India Hicks, granddaughter of the late Lord Mountbatten, so named through the family's connections with the country.

INDIRA—**f** 'Beauty' (Hindu, from Sanskrit). Indira Gandhi (1917-84), Prime Minister of India assassinated in 1984.

INDRAYAN—**m** (Hindu). From Indra, god of the air and the sky.

INEZ, INÉZ—**f** Spanish form of Agnes.

INGRAM—**m** 'Anglian raven' or 'Ing's raven' (Teutonic). Derivation from the surname.

INGRID—**f** 'Fair one of Ing [the Fertility God]' (Old Norse). Most influenced by Ingrid Bergman (1915-82), Swedish-born actress.

INIGO—**m** Medieval Spanish form of Ignatius. Inigo Jones (1573-1652), English architect.

INNES—**m** 'Island' (Gaelic) Place-name/surname derivation.

IOLANTHE—**f** Popularised by Gilbert and Sullivan's light opera of that name (1882) but rarely used now.

IONA—**f** From the Hebridean island, early centre of Christianity.

IRA—**m** 'Watchful' (Hebrew). One of the priests of King David of Israel. Ira Gershwin (1896-1983) wrote the lyrics for many of his brother George's songs.

IRAM—**m** 'Crown of the head' (Arabic).

IRENE—**f** 'Peace' (Greek). Eighth-century Byzantine empress. Late use in England although it was the name of four early saints.

IRIS—**f** 'Rainbow' (Greek). Another example of the flower names which were so popular by the end of the nineteenth century.

IRVING—**m** Form of Irwin.

IRWIN—**m** 'Respected friend' (Old English).

ISAAC—**m** 'God may laugh with me' (Hebrew). Sarah laughed when told that she would bear Isaac in her old age. Sir Isaac Newton (1642-1727), first propounder of the principle of gravity. Izaak Walton (1593-1683), the 'father of angling' and author of *The Compleat Angler*.

ISABEL, ISABELLA—**f** Interchangeable with Elizabeth, of which it is a French variant. Isabella Beaton wrote the famous cookery book.

ISADORA—**f** Form of Isidore. Isadora Duncan (1878-1927), 'American aesthetic dancer', was an eccentric of her time.

ISAIAH—**m** 'God is salvation' (Hebrew). Hebrew prophet.

ISAMBARD—**m** Surname derivation. A possible interpretation as the Teutonic or Old English for 'iron-bright' would make it a fitting name for Isambard Kingdom Brunel (1806-59), famous engineer of the Industrial Revolution.

ISIDORE—**m** 'God's gift' (Greek). St Isidore of Seville (died 636), Spanish encyclopaedist and bishop.

ISLA—**f** (Scottish). Recently introduced, possibly from Islay, the island.

ISOLDA—**f** Of German origin: the name of the heroine in the Tristan romances; used here in the latinised form made popular through Wagner's opera *Tristan und Isolde*.

ISRAEL—**m** 'May God prevail' or 'he who struggles with God' (Hebrew). The name given to Jacob after he overcame the angel (Genesis 32: 28); thus the twelve tribes of Israel were named after his sons.

IVAN—**m** Scottish form of Ivo. The name of a line of Dukes of Moscow, later Tsars of Russia, including Ivan the Terrible (1530-84).

IVO—**m** 'Yew wood' (Teutonic), by implication meaning 'archer'. A name which came over with William the Conqueror as the French Yves, already common in heroic literature.

IVOR—**m** 'Bow-bearer' (Teutonic). From the Old Norse name of tenth-century Danish kings of Dublin.

IVY—**f** Flower name.

JABBAR—**m** 'Mighty, powerful' (Muslim).

JABEZ—**m** 'Sorrow' (Hebrew). Indicating that the child was born during some period of distress for family or tribe.

JACALYN—**f** Modern invented name based on Jacqueline.

JACARANDA—**f** Name of the tropical American tree with blue blossom.

JACINTH—**f** Derivative of Hyacinth. In modern use denotes an orange-red variety of zircon.

JACK—**m** Pet form of John. Used independently even from medieval times.

JACLINA—**f** 'Comely' (Greek).

JACOB—**m** 'Taking by the heel' (Hebrew). Referring originally to the birth of one of the twin sons of Isaac and Rebecca, who supposedly grabbed his brother Esau's heel (Genesis 25: 33).

JACQUELINE—**f** Feminine and diminutive form of the French Jacques, English James.

JACQUETTA—**f** Feminine diminutive of Jacques. Jacquetta Hawkes, archaeologist.

JADE—**f** Modern introduction from the semi-precious stone. Daughter of Mick Jagger, rock singer since the 1960s.

JAGO—**m** Cornish form of James developed from the surname.

JAIME—**f** Made up from the French *j'aime*, 'I love'.

JAKE—**m** Short form of Jacob now used as a separate name.

JALAJAA—**f** 'Lotus blossom' (Hindu).

JALAL—**m** 'Glory' (Muslim).

JALEEL—**m** 'Great, fine' (Muslim). Also as Jalila.

JAMAL—**m** 'Handsome' (Arabic). Used more in USA though it is current in some immigrant communities in Britain.

JAMES—**m** Derives from Jacob, via the late Latin form Iacomus. Jacob was retained as the name of the Old Testament tribal leader and James was used for the two apostles of the New Testament. Borne by five kings of Scotland and two of both England and Scotland.

JAMESINA—**f** The original female form of James, nowadays shortened to Jaime (with implication *j'aime* – 'I love') or to Jamie.

JAMIE—**m** Affectionate diminutive of James.

JAN—**m** Northern European form of John. Also occurs in West Country dialect.

JANCIS—**f** Recent invention combining Jane and Frances.

JANE—**f** A rendering of Joan very common since the eighteenth century.

JANELLE, JANEL, JANELL—**f** Diminutives of Jane started in USA around 1950.

JANET—**f** Diminutive of Jane.

JANICE—**f** Modern development of Jane. First occurs in *Janice Meredith*, published in 1899.

JANINE—**f** Invented from the sound of the French Jeannine.

JANITA—**f** Derived as an English form of Juanita, Spanish feminine of John.

JAPHET—**m** 'May his tribe increase' (Hebrew). Third son of Noah and reputed ancestor of the Indo-European race.

JAQUMINE—**f** Combination of two names, Jacqueline and Jasmine.

JARED—**m** 'Servant' (Accadian). Father of Enoch (Genesis 5: 15-20). Used by Puritans in seventeenth-century England, now undergoing a revival.

JARITA—**f** 'Bird of legend' (Hindi).

JARVIS—**m** Form of Gervais.

JASMINE—**f** Flower name, originally Persian Yasmin.

JASON—**m** Meaning unknown. In Greek legend, leader of the Argonauts in their quest for the Golden Fleece.

JASPAR, JASPER—**m** 'Keeper of the treasure' (Persian). An alternative form of Gaspar, one of the Three Wise Men who went to Bethlehem to pay homage to the infant Jesus.

JAWAHARLAL—**m** 'Victory' (Hindu). Jawaharlal Nehru (1889-1964), first Prime Minister of India.

JAY—**m** Modern derivation from the bird or from the phonetic spelling of the letter J.

JAYMEE—**f** A recent invention based on James.

JAYNE—**f** A modern spelling of Jane.

JEAN—**f** A modern Scottish form, through Jane, of Joan.

JEANETTE—**f** French diminutive of Jeanne (French feminine form of John), now used as a separate name.

JEANNINE, JEANINE—**f** Diminutive of Jean (the French form of John). A range of spellings includes Jenine and Janine.

JED—**m** Short form of Jedidiah, 'friend of God' (Hebrew). One of the names applied to Solomon.

JEFFERY, JEFFREY—**m** Forms of Geoffrey.

JELENA—**f** Modern invented name.

JEMIMA—**f** 'Dove' (Hebrew). One of the three daughters of Job.

JEMMA—**f** A modern, phonetic spelling of Gemma.

JENA—**f** 'Patience' (Hindu).

JENKIN—**m** From early English and Welsh forename (adminutive of Jan) and surname.

JENNA—**f** Diminutive form of Jane or Jenny.

JENNET—**f** English variant of Jeanette.

JENNIFER—**f** Cornish form of Guinevere, wife of King Arthur.

JENNY—**f** Pet-name for Jane or short form of Jennifer which has been used in its own right, as in Jenny Lind (1820-87), 'The Swedish Nightingale'.

JEREMIAH—**m** 'May God exalt' (Hebrew). Second of the greater prophets of Israel. Jeremiah Clarke (1674-1707), English composer credited with well-known 'Trumpet Voluntary'.

JEREMY—**m** Form of Jeremiah. Jeremy Bentham (1748-1832), political philosopher.

JERMYN—**m** Originally from Latin *Germanus* ('German').

JEROME—**m** 'Holy name' (Greek). St Jerome (340-420), one of the 'fathers' of the early church, translated the Bible into the vulgar language (Latin) of the time, and it is still called the Vulgate Bible. Jerome K. Jerome (1859-1927), author of *Three Men in a Boat*.

JERRY—**m** Affectionate form of Gerald or Jeremy used as a separate name.

JESSE—**m** 'God exists' (Hebrew). Father of David, King of Israel.

JESSICA—**f** 'He beholds' (Hebrew). Of ancient lineage, but its modern use is traced to Shakespeare's *Merchant of Venice*.

JESSIE—**f** Though obviously a short form of Jessica, its true origin is as a pet-name for Janet.

JETHRO—**m** 'Abundant virtues' (Hebrew). Jethro Tull (1674-1741), farmer and writer on agriculture.

JETTA—**f** Invented elaboration of jet, the semi-precious stone.

JEWEL—**f** A 'precious stone' name.

JILL—**f** Form of Gillian now quite independent.

JIVAN—**m** 'Life' (Hindu).

JOACHIM—**m** 'May God exalt' (Hebrew). Reputed father of the Virgin Mary.

JOAN—**f** Form of John. By the sixteenth century one of the commonest English female names.

JOANNA, JOHANNA—**f** A medieval rendering into Latin of Joan, reintroduced in the eighteenth century.

JOANNE—**f** Recent combination of diminutive of Josephine and Anne.

JOB—**m** 'Persecuted' or 'weeper' (Hebrew). A long-suffering figure in the Old Testament.

JOCASTA—**f** The ill-fated mother of Oedipus in Greek mythology.

JOCELYN, JOSCELIN—**m** or **f** 'One of the Gothic clan' (Teutonic). A Norman introduction. Jocelin de Brakelond (1155-1215), a monk at Bury St Edmunds, wrote a lively account of life at the abbey there.

JODIE, JODI, JODY—**f** Affectionate forms of Judith.

JOEL—**m** 'Jehovah is God' (Hebrew). Introduced into England by the Normans.

JOELLE—**f** French feminine of Joel becoming popular in English.

JOHN—**m** 'Whom God favours' (Hebrew). John the Baptist was cousin and forerunner of Jesus. St John, author of the fourth gospel. There have been at least 23 popes of this name and an infinite number of rulers of countries all round the world. 'John Bull' represents the typical Englishman.

JOLENE—**f** Recent invention from USA influenced by its use as the title of a song sung by Dolly Parton and recorded in 1979.

JOLYON—**m** A form of Julian. A character in Galsworthy's *Forsyte Saga* (1906-22).

JONAH, JONAS—**m** 'Dove' (Hebrew). Hebrew prophet featuring in the story of the whale.

JONATHAN—**m** 'God's gift' (Hebrew). Son of King Saul. His particular friendship with David gave the phrase 'a David and Jonathan' to describe close companions.

JONELLA—**f** American invention from the old names John and Ella.

JONQUIL—**f** A fragrant narcissus with several pale blooms on one stalk. Flower name of modern use.

JORAM—**m** 'The Lord is exalted' (Hebrew).

JORDAN—**m** From the holy river, probably because the child was baptised in water brought especially from that river.

JOSEPH—**m** 'God granted' (Hebrew). Son of Jacob and Rachel. Husband of the Virgin Mary.

JOSEPHINE—**f** Form of Joseph. Napoleon's Empress Josephine started the modern interest. Fifi is a pet form.

JOSHUA—**m** 'God is my strength' (Hebrew). Jesus is a form of this name. Joshua succeeded Moses and led the Israelites to the Promised Land. Sir Joshua Reynolds (1723-92) was first President of the Royal Academy.

JOSIAH—**m** 'Bring healing' (Hebrew). King of Judah about 600 BC. Josiah Wedgwood (1730-95), the famous potter.

JOSS—**m** or **f** Shortened form of Jocelyn now used separately.

JOY—**f** Originally denoting the emotion felt by a mother on the birth of her baby.

JOYCE—**m** or **f** First appears in Celtic as Jodoc, a seventh-century Breton saint. Used for men at first but now largely a feminine preserve, perhaps through the heroine of Edna Lyall's very popular *In the Golden Days* (1885).

JUAN—**m** Spanish form of John now sometimes used in English-speaking world.

JUDE—**m** 'Guided by God' (Hebrew). Judah, leader of the tribe which later formed the kingdom, is the origin of the word Jew. As Judas its connection with Iscariot made it most unpopular. Today's revival may be based on film and television productions of Thomas Hardy's *Jude the Obscure* (1895).

JUDITH—**f** 'A Jewess' (Hebrew). Old Testament figure who seduced and killed Holofernes, an enemy general. King Aethelwulf (died 878) married Judith, daughter of Charles the Bald.

JUDY—**f** Short form of Judith. Judy Garland (1922-69), star of *The Wizard of Oz* and other films.

JULIA—**f** Form of Julius. Daughter of Julius Caesar. Appears in Shakespeare's *Two Gentlemen of Verona*. Robert Herrick (1591-1674) addressed many of his poems to 'Julia'.

JULIAN—**m** Form of Julius. St Julian the Hospitaller is one of the patron saints of travellers.

JULIANA—**f** Form of Julian. Juliana Berners, fourteenth-century prioress said to have written the *Boke of St Albans*, one of the earliest books on hunting and fishing. Juliana, queen of the Netherlands who abdicated in favour of her daughter Beatrix in 1980.

JULIE—**f** Diminutive of Julia.

JULIET—**f** Remote form of Julius. Its popularity entirely due to Shakespeare's *Romeo and Juliet*.

JULIETTE—**f** French form of Juliet.

JULIUS—**m** Great Roman family name, as in Caius Julius Caesar, possibly from Greek *ioules,* 'downy [bearded]'. Sir Julius Caesar was the adopted name of an Italian physician to Queen Elizabeth I.

JUMANAH—**f** 'Pearl' (Muslim).

JUNE—**f** Name of the month. A recent innovation.

JUNIPER—**m** or **f** From the name of the shrub, used from at least as early as the eighteenth century.

JUSTIN—**m** Anglicised form of Latin Justus 'just'. Name of two Byzantine emperors. St Justin, philosopher of the second century.

JUSTINA—**f** Form of Justin. A fourth-century saint.

JUSTINIAN—**m** Derives from Justin. Sixth- and seventh-century Byzantine emperors.

JYOTI—**f** 'Light' (Hindi).

KALA—**f** 'Black' (Hindi). Referring to colour of hair.

KALI—**f** 'Energy' (Sanskrit).

KALILA—**f** 'Beloved' (Arabic).

KAMAL—**m** 'Perfection' (Muslim).

KAMANIKA—**f** 'Beautiful' (Hindu).

KANTI—**f** 'Loveliness' (Hindu).

KANU—**m** 'Beautiful' (Hindu).

KANYA—**f** 'Young lady' (Thai).

KARA—**f** 'Dear' (Greek).

KAREEM—**m** 'Generous, noble' (Muslim). Also spelt Karim.

KAREL—**m** Dutch and Czech form of Charles.

KAREN—**f** Form of Catherine, from Denmark and now popular.

KARL—**m** 'A man' (Teutonic). German and Scandinavian form of Charles now becoming popular as an English name, with the feminine form Karla.

KASTURBA—**f** 'Musk' (Hindu). The wife of Mahatma Gandhi.

KATARINA—**f** Swedish form of Catherine.

KATE—**f** Short form of Catherine used independently since the middle ages. Shakespeare's leading character in *The Taming of the Shrew*.

KATHARINE, KATHERINE—**f** Variants of Catherine.

KATHLEEN—**f** Irish form of Catherine.

KATHRYN—**f** Americanised variation of Catherine.

KATINKA—**f** Russian diminutive of Katya meaning Catherine.

KATRINA, KATRIONA—**f** Forms of Catherine.

KAY—**f** Pet-name for Catherine now used independently.

KAYLA—**f** 'Crown' (Hebrew).

KAYLEY—**f** From the Irish surname, originally a personal name indicating slimness of figure.

KEAN—**m** 'Warrior' (Manx).

KEELEY—**f** Recent Irish introduction, perhaps as a variant of Kayley.

KEIR—**m** From the surname, a variant of Kerr. James Keir Hardie (1856-1915), first Labour MP. It was his mother's maiden name.

KEITH—**m** 'Of the wood' (Gaelic). Originally a place-name.

KELLY—**m** or **f** Anglicised form of Irish; Gaelic for 'war'; may also relate to Cornish for 'wood'. More used for girls than for boys.

KELSEY—**m** or **f** 'Ship of victory' (Old English). A man who had commanded a ship which won a battle at sea got this personal name.

KELVIN—**m** First used in 1920s. Influenced perhaps by fame of Lord Kelvin (1824-1907), Scottish mathematician and scientist, and by the name of a river which runs into the Clyde.

KENDRICK, KENRICK—**m** Originally a surname, the meaning of which is uncertain but could refer to a chief.

KENELM—**m** 'Bold helmet' (Old English). King of Mercia murdered in 819 and canonised.

KENNEDY—**m** From an Irish Gaelic root, meaning 'ugly head'. Used for centuries as a surname.

KENNETH—**m** Probably from Gaelic *caioneach,* 'handsome'. First king of Scotland (died 860).

KENTON—**m** Originally place-name, then surname. Used in radio serial *The Archers.*

KERENHAPPUCH—**f** 'Horn of stibium' (Hebrew), which rephrased means 'pot of eye makeup'! Often shortened to Keren. Refers to predilection of one of the daughters of Job, who was given this name.

KERMIT—**m** An old Irish surname used by Theodore Roosevelt to name one of his sons. Made known world-wide by the frog puppet created for *The Muppet Show* by Jim Henson (1936-90).

KERRY—**m** From Irish Gaelic *ciarda,* 'dark'.

KETURAH—**f** 'Fragrance' (Hebrew).

KEVIN—**m** From Irish Gaelic *caomhghin,* 'gentle and loved'. An Irish saint, sixth-century abbot of Glandalough.

KEZIAH—**f** 'Cinammon' (Hebrew). One of the daughters of Job.

KHALIL—**m** (Muslim) 'Friend'.

KIA, KIANA—**f** See Quiana.

KICKI—**f** Swedish diminutive of Kristina. Used in English perhaps to record baby's liveliness in the womb.

KIERAN—**m** Anglicised form of Ciarán.

KIM—**m** or **f** Short form of Kimball, 'war-chief' (Celtic), and of Kimberley; now used independently. Central character in novel *Kim* (1901) by Rudyard Kipling.

KIMBERLEY—**m** or **f** From a place-name in England which named a family of whom a peer gave that name to the gold town of Kimberley in South Africa.

KINGDOM—**m** Surname derivation, rarely used. Isambard Kingdom Brunel (1806-59), the famous engineer, was son of Sophie Kingdom, married to Marc Brunel.

KINGSLEY—**m** 'King's wood' (English). Dwelling place gave rise to personal name which became surname.

KIRSTIE, KIRSTY—**f** Scottish diminutive of Kirstin now used throughout English-speaking world as an independent name.

KIT—**m** or **f** Short form of Christopher or Catherine.

KITA—**f** Pet-name for Catherine now used independently.

KITTY—**f** Short form of Catherine.

KORA, KORE—**f** 'Girl' (Greek). Less common in English than its variant Cora. Kora was another name given to Proserpina.

KRISHNA—**m** 'Delightful' (Hindu).

KRYSTLE—**f** Form of Crystal used for a character in the television series *Dynasty*.

KUSHALI—**f** 'Clever' (Hindu).

KYLIE—**f** Started in Australia, said to be derived from an Aborigine word for boomerang. Kylie Minogue, Australian actress and singer (born 1969), influenced its popularity world-wide.

LACEY—**m** English place-name/surname origin.

LACHLAN—**m** 'Warlike' (Gaelic).

LAETITIA, LETITIA—**f** 'Joy' (Latin). Name of asteroid number 39.

LAKSHA—**f** 'White rose' (Hindu).

LAKSHMAN—**m** (Hindi). The younger brother of Ram.

LAKSHMI—**f** 'Lucky' (Hindu).

LALAGE—**f** 'Merry talk' (Greek).

LALIKA—**f** 'Beautiful woman' (Hindu from Sanskrit).

LALITA—**f** 'Playful, charming' (Hindu).

LAMBERT—**m** 'Of the bright land' (Teutonic). Lambert Simnel (1475-1537) was pretender to the throne of England.

LANA—**f** An invention first used by actress Lana Turner (born 1920).

LANCE—**m** Short form of Lancelot.

LANCELOT—**m** Uncertain Celtic derivation, but influenced by French. One of the most famous of the legendary knights of the Round Table. Lancelot ('Capability') Brown (1716-83), landscape gardener.

LANGLEY—**m** 'Long meadow' (Old English). Developed from the common place-name.

LARA—**f** Short form of Larissa. Popularised by character in Boris Pasternak's *Dr Zhivago* (1957) and the film of 1965 with its music 'Lara's Theme'.

LARISSA—f (Russian). Origin unknown. May be from the ancient Thessalonian town of this name.

LATASHA—f Invented name popular in the USA.

LAURA—f Probably derives from Laurence. The subject of Petrarch's sonnets of the fourteenth century. Dame Laura Knight (1877-1970), English artist.

LAUREL—f Popular Victorian plant name, from the shrub.

LAUREN—f Variant of Laura. Lauren Bacall (born 1924), actress and widow of Humphrey Bogart.

LAURENCE, LAWRENCE—m 'Of the city of Laurentum' (Latin) or from Latin *laurus*, 'laurel', symbol of the conquering hero. St Laurence, Christian martyr in 258.

LAVENDER—f The popular sweet-smelling herb.

LAVINIA—f 'Of Lavinium [a town near Rome]' (Latin). Lavinia was the second wife of Aeneas. Thomson's translation of the book of Ruth described her as 'the lovely young Lavinia' and brought it into favour.

LEAH—f 'Languid' (Hebrew). First wife of Jacob (Genesis 29: 31). Although Leah was 'tender-eyed', Jacob preferred her younger sister Rachel. Became 36th most popular girls' name after death of Leah Betts, teenager who died after taking the drug 'ecstacy'.

LEANDER—m The Greek who, according to legend, swam across the Hellespont and back each day to see his beloved Hero.

LEANNE, LIANNE—f Developed as an affectionate form of Juliana but can also be conjunction of Lee and Anne, especially in USA.

LEE—m Short form of Leo or from the surname.

LEIGH—m 'Meadow' (Old English). Leigh Hunt (1784-1859), essayist and poet.

LEILA—f From the name of the heroine of the popular Persian tale 'Leila and Majnun'.

LEMUEL—m 'A man for God' (Hebrew). A king mentioned in Proverbs. The hero (Lemuel Gulliver) of Jonathan Swift's *Gulliver's Travels* (1726).

LENA—f Short form of Helen.

LENNOX—m Surname/place-name derivation.

LEO—m 'Lion' (Latin). The name of six emperors of Constantinople and thirteen popes.

LEONARD—m 'Bold as a lion' (Teutonic). The patron saint of prisoners. Leonardo da Vinci (1452-1519), great Italian painter and inventor.

LEONIE—f French form of Leo.

LEONORA—f Form of Eleanor introduced from the continent after the popularity of Beethoven's opera *Fidelio* (1814), which was first called *Leonora* after its heroine.

LEOPOLD—m 'Brave among people' (Teutonic). Victorian use through the queen's uncle Leopold, King of the Belgians, after whom she named her third son.

LEROY—m 'The king' (French).

LESHEM—f 'Precious stone' (Hebrew).

LESLEY—f Form of Leslie. Robert Burns wrote the poem 'Bonnie Lesley' to Miss Lesley Baillie.

LESLIE—m or **f** Deriving through a surname from a place-name.

LESTER—m Originally a place-name.

LETTICE—f English form of Laetitia. Lettice Knollys was wife of the Earl of Essex in Elizabeth I's reign.

LETTY—f Diminutive of Alethea or Lettice.

LEVI—m 'Promised' (Hebrew). Third son of Jacob and Leah.

LEWIS, LOUIS—m Derived from Ludwig, 'famous warrior' (Teutonic). As Louis, French kings from Louis the Pious, born 778, to Louis-Phillippe, died in exile in 1850. Lewis Carroll, author of *Alice's Adventures in Wonderland* (1865).

LEX—m Short form of Alex(ander), now used as a separate name.

LIAM—m Irish form of William. It had a meteoric rise in use with the reputation of Oasis singer Liam Gallagher, 1996-7.

LIANNE—f See Leanne.

LIBBY—f Diminutive of Elizabeth now used in its own right.

LIESE—f German short form of Elizabeth now popular as an English name.

LILAC—f One of the plant names.

LILIAN, LILLAH, LILLY—f Forms of Elizabeth, though found separately from an early date; modern parents may have the lily in mind.

LILIAS—f Form of Lilian. Daughter of Rider Haggard, authoress in her own right.

LILITH—f The Assyro-Babylonian goddess of storms.

LILY—f Very old-established plant name, symbol of purity.

LINCOLN—m English place-name/surname derivation.

LINDA—f 'Serpent' (Teutonic) or 'pretty' (Spanish).

LINDON—m See Lyndon.

LINDSAY, LINDSEY—m or **f** Surname/place-name origin, but re-imported as a Christian name from the United States.

LINFORD—m See under Lynford.

LINNET—f Possibly derives from the Welsh Eluned, but more likely borrowed directly from the bird.

LINTON—m Place-name/surname derivation.

LINUS—m 'Flaxen hair' (Greek). Character in the comic strip 'Peanuts'.

LINZI—**f** Invented name based on Lindsay.

LIONEL—**m** Medieval diminutive of Leo. Name given to the third son (1330-80) of Edward III, who was made Duke of Clarence.

LISA—**f** Short form of Elizabeth.

LISBET—**f** Short form of Elizabeth now used independently.

LISE—**f** German short form of Elizabeth.

LIVIA—**f** Roman family name.

LLEWELLYN—**m** 'Leader' (Welsh). Llywelyn (died 1240), son of Iorwerth, Prince of All Wales, married a daughter of England's King John.

LLOYD—**m** 'Grey' (Welsh). David Lloyd George, British Prime Minister 1916-22.

LOBELIA—**f** Modern plant name.

LOGAN—**m** Surname derivation from the Ayrshire place-name.

LOGIE—**m** Surname derivation. Made famous by John Logie Baird (1888-1946), television pioneer who gave the first demonstration of a television image in 1926.

LOIS—**f** Possibly a Greek name. The name of Timothy's grandmother in II Timothy 1:5.

LOLA—**f** (Spanish). Diminutive of Dolores.

LORA—**f** Another spelling of Laura.

LORELLE—**f** American elaboration of Laura.

LORETTA—**f** 'From Loreto', a famous place of pilgrimage (Italian). Loretta Young, American actress.

LORNA—**f** Invented by R. D. Blackmore for the heroine of *Lorna Doone* in 1869.

LORRAINE—**f** French place-name.

LOUELLA—**f** Modern American invention based on Louise. Louella Parsons (1880-1972), famed Hollywood gossip columnist.

LOUIS—**m** See under Lewis.

LOUISE, LOUISA—**f** Forms of Louis. Louise, supplanted at one time by Louisa, is again the more popular today.

LOVEDAY—**f** Used in early times for a child born on a day when the family had made an agreeable settlement in business or family affairs.

LOVELL, LOWELL—**m** A diminutive of Louve, 'wolf' (Anglo-Norman).

LUCAS—**m** Form of Luke. Surname derivation.

LUCASTA—**f** Invented by Richard Lovelace (1618-57), Cavalier poet, as the object of his verses.

LUCIA, LUCY—**f** Forms of Lucius. Patron saint of those who suffer from 'distemper of the eyes', St Lucy was killed in 303.

LUCIAN, LUCIEN—**m** Forms of Lucius. Lucian was a second-century Greek satirist.

LUCILLA, LUCILLE—f Diminutive forms of Lucius.

LUCINDA—f Romantic form of Lucy.

LUCIUS—m Derived from Latin *lux,* 'light'. Lucius was pope 253-4. Lucius Apuleius, versatile Latin writer AD *c.*150.

LUCRETIA—f Roman family name. In legend Lucretia, raped by Sextus Tarquinius, killed herself. Lucrezia Borgia (1480-1519), legendary wanton, cast a shadow on the name.

LUCY—f See under Lucia.

LUDOVIC—m Latinised form of Ludwig. See under Lewis.

LUKE—m Anglicised form of the biblical name meaning 'of Lucania' (Greek). St Luke, author of the third gospel, patron saint of painters and physicians.

LULIE—f Further diminutive of Lucy or Lulu.

LULU—f Diminutive of Louise and Lucy.

LUTHER—m 'People's warrior' or 'people's army' (Teutonic). Martin Luther (1483-1546), German religious reformer and translator of the Bible.

LYCORIS—f 'Twilight' (Greek). Remembering time of birth.

LYDIA—f 'Woman of Lydia' (Greek). Lydia Languish is the heroine of Sheridan's *The Rivals* (1775).

LYN, LYNNE—f Form of the Welsh name Eluned. As Lynn occasionally used as a male name.

LYNDON—m Derived from a surname meaning 'lime-tree hill' (Old English).

LYNETTE—f From Old French Linette, 'linnet'. Used by Tennyson in his *Idylls of the King* (1872).

LYNFORD, LINFORD—m Norfolk place-name/surname origin. Linford Christie, Olympic sprinter.

LYSANDER—m 'Champion of freedom' (Greek).

LYTTON—m Surname derivation from place-name. Lytton Strachey (1880-1932), author of *Eminent Victorians* (1918).

MABEL—f A short form of Amabel. Mab, Queen of the Fairies, is first mentioned in Shakespeare's *Romeo and Juliet*.

MABYN—f 'Youthful' (Welsh).

MADELEINE—f 'Woman of Magdala' (Hebrew). From Mary Magdalene, a friend of Christ.

MADGE—f Short form of Margaret, used independently.

MADHU—**f** 'Sweet and beautiful' (Hindu). Also the first month of the Indian year.

MADOC—**m** 'Lucky' (Welsh). Twelfth-century Welsh prince, subject of a poem by Southey. Ford Madox Ford (1873-1939), novelist.

MADONNA—**f** 'My lady' (Old Italian). Also the Italian name for the Mother of Christ. Made popular in the USA through the pop star Madonna Ciccone (born 1959).

MAE—**f** Origin unknown, possibly from May or Maeve. Film star Mae West (1892-1980).

MAEVE—**f** 'Intoxicating' (Gaelic). Name of legendary queen of Connacht in the epic 'The Cattle Raid of Cooley'.

MAGDA—**f** German short form of Magdalen or Madeleine.

MAGDALEN—**f** Form of Madeleine.

MAGDI—**f** 'My glory' (Arabic).

MAGGIE—**f** Short form of Margaret.

MAGNOLIA—**f** Flower name.

MAGNUS—**m** 'Great' (Latin). King Magnus I of Norway and Denmark, died 1047.

MAHALAH—**f** 'Tenderness' (Hebrew). Also a Hebrew place-name. *Mehalah* (1880) by Sabine Baring-Gould reflects the use of this name in Essex at that time.

MAIDIE—**f** Simply meant the 'little maid' when used in Gilbert and Sullivan's *Iolanthe* (1882), but it was taken as a genuine forename by some listeners and used for their children.

MAIR, MAIRE—**f** Welsh and Irish forms of Mary.

MAISIE—**f** From the Gaelic form of Margaret.

MAJA, MAYA—**f** Possibly from the Maya Indians of South America. Used from 1980s, mostly by Americans.

MAJID, MADJID—**m** 'Glory' (Hindu).

MAJOR—**m** Surname origin. Brothers at public school were called Major and Minor (Latin for 'larger' and 'smaller') in order to distinguish them. Now it has a fanciful use, largely in the USA.

MAJORIE—**f** Looks like a misspelling of Marjorie but was intended as a feminine form of Major.

MALACHI—**m** 'Messenger' (Hebrew). Translator of the Old Testament book named it from a passage saying 'Behold I send Malachi', which should have been translated as 'my messenger'!

MALATI—**f** 'Moonlight' (Hindu). Remembering time of baby's birth.

MALCOLM—**m** 'Columba's disciple' (Gaelic). Very common in Scotland, after four kings, ruling from 943 to 1165.

MALDWYN—**m** (Welsh). The native name for Montgomeryshire, thus a surname from which the forename derives.

MALIK—**m** 'King' (Muslim).

MALIKA—**f** 'Queen' (Muslim).

MALLORY—**m** Surname derivation. Used occasionally even though the original French word *malheureux* means 'unfortunate'.

MALVIN—**m** A variant of Melvin.

MALVINA—**f** 'Smooth-browed' (Gaelic). It appears that this name is wholly the invention of James Macpherson for his *Poems of Ossian* (1762).

MAMIE—**f** American diminutive of Mary.

MANDY—**f** Short form of Amanda or Miranda, now used independently.

MANFRED—**m** 'Man of peace' (Teutonic).

MANLEY—**m** From early surname meaning 'common field' though the name might also reflect the manliness of its bearer. Gerard Manley Hopkins (1844-89), priest and poet.

MANSOOR—**m** 'Victorious' (Muslim).

MANUEL—**m** Spanish form of Emanuel.

MANUELA, MANUELLA—**f** Spanish forms of Emanuel.

MARA—**f** 'Bitter' (Hebrew). From the book of Ruth 1:20: '… call me Mara for the Almighty has dealt very bitterly with me.'

MARBELLA—**f** Short form of Mariabella, 'beautiful Mary' (Latin).

MARCELLA—**f** Form of Marcellus.

MARCELLUS—**m** Diminutive of Marcus.

MARCENE—**f** American development of Marcia which had some popularity in the 1940s.

MARCIA—**f** Form of Marcus.

MARCO—**m** Italian form of Mark.

MARCONI—**m** or **f** Surname of Guglielmo Marconi (1874-1937), Italian pioneer of radio telegraphy and the first radio station in the world. Given to a girl born in 1911 as her third forename.

MARCUS—**m** Could be linked to Marius. The Latin name of the second evangelist.

MARDI—**f** 'Tuesday' (French). Occasionally used for a girl born on this day.

MARELLA—**f** Combination of Mary and Ella which was in circulation as early as 1930.

MARETTA—**f** A variant of the French Mariette, used as a diminutive of English Mary.

MARGARET—**f** 'Pearl' (Greek). St Margaret, beheaded in 275, is patron saint of expectant mothers. A royal name through the ages in nearly every country in Europe.

MARGERY, MARJORIE—**f** French pet forms of Margaret, used separately in England since the thirteenth century.

MARGOT—**f** Separate name coined from Marguerite.

MARGUERITE—**f** French form of Margaret, also meaning 'daisy'.

MARIA—**f** Latin form of Mary used in many languages, notably Italian and Spanish. One of the most popular names in the Christian world.

MARIAN—**f** Diminutive of Mary. Popularised by the legend of Robin Hood and Maid Marian. See also Marion.

MARIANNE—**f** French form of Marian or Miriam.

MARIBEL—**f** Short form of Spanish Maria Isabel.

MARIE—**f** French form of Mary and Maria.

MARIETTA, MARIETTE—**f** Diminutive of Marie becoming popular in Britain, perhaps from the young heroine in H. E. Bates's *Darling Buds of May* as adapted for television.

MARIGOLD—**f** Flower-name of recent adoption.

MARIKA—**f** (Slavonic). Affectionate form of Maria now used independently.

MARILYN—**f** Modern version of Mary, also a combination of Mary and Lyn. Made popular through Marilyn Monroe (1926-62), much idolised film actress.

MARINA—**f** 'Of the sea' (Latin). Princess Marina (1906-68) married George, Duke of Kent, in 1934.

MARION—**f** or **m** From the early French form of Marie.

MARISSA—**f** Uncommon diminutive of Mary.

MARIUS—**m** 'Of Mars' (Latin). Roman family name.

MARJORIE—**f** See under Margery.

MARK—**m** English form of Marcus. St Mark, author of the second gospel.

MARLENE—**f** Short form of Mary Magdalene.

MARLOW—**m** Derives through an early surname from the place in Buckinghamshire.

MARMADUKE—**m** 'Servant of Maedoc' (Irish). An Anglo-Norman interpretation of the Irish, which has remained locally in the north of England.

MARTHA—**f** 'Noble lady' (Aramaic). The sister of Mary and Lazarus in the Bible. Canonised as the patron saint of housewives.

MARTIN—**m** From Latin name Martinus, which probably relates to the God Mars. St Martin of Tours, soldier-bishop of the fourth century, remembered in St Martin-in-the-Fields church in London.

MARVIN—**m** Derived from Merfin, ninth-century king of Wales (Old Welsh).

MARY—**f** New-Testament form of Miriam. The mother of Jesus, and so too holy to be much used in early days; but the very devotion of the common people brought it into frequent use.

MASOOD—**m** 'Contented, happy' (Muslim); also spelt Masud.

MATILDA—**f** 'Strength in adversity' (Teutonic). Wife of William the Conqueror.

MATTHEW—**f** 'Gift of God' (Hebrew). St Matthew, author of the first gospel. Captain Matthew Webb, first man to swim the English Channel (1875).

MATTHIAS—**m** Form of Matthew used to distinguish the disciple who took the place of Judas Iscariot.

MAUD, MAUDE—**f** A form of Matilda introduced from France very early. Revived through Tennyson's 'Maud' (1855).

MAURA—**f** Irish form of Mary.

MAUREEN—**f** Irish diminutive of Mary taken up by Americans and revived in England.

MAURICE—**m** 'A Moor' (Greek). St Maurice, third-century martyr.

MAVIS—**f** The old name for the song thrush, possibly introduced by Marie Corelli for a character in *The Sorrows of Satan* (1895).

MAXIMILIAN—**m** 'Greatest' (Latin). The name is said to have been invented by the Holy Roman Emperor Frederick III (1415-93), hoping that his son would combine the virtues of two great Romans: Quintus Fabius Maximus and Scipio Aemilianus. So the name was used in German ruling families down to the twentieth century. Used more often in its abbreviated form of Max.

MAXINE—**f** Popular French name which came to Britain via the USA.

MAXWELL—**m** Place-name/surname origin.

MAY—**f** Short form of Margaret or Mary, but also standing for the month in which the child was born.

MAYBELL—**f** Invented name possibly from Mabel or from May and Belle.

MAYNARD—**m** 'Strong and enduring' (Teutonic). Became a surname very early on. John Maynard Keynes (1883-1946), economist.

MEAVE—**f** 'The merry one' (Irish). The folk heroine later chronicled as queen of the Irish fairies.

MEDWIN—**m** May mean 'drinking companion' or 'fellow labourer' (Old English).

MEENA—**f** 'Precious' (Hindu). Name of the daughter of Usha, the goddess of the dawn.

MEG—**f** Short form of Margaret now used independently. Meg March, one of the characters in *Little Women* (1868) by Louisa M. Alcott.

MEGAN—**f** Welsh pet form of Margaret.

MEGARA—**f** (Greek). First wife of Hercules.

MEHITABEL—**f** 'Whom God hath chosen' (Hebrew).

MEIR—**m** 'Giving light' (Hebrew).

MEL—**m** or **f** Short form of Melvin, Melville, Melanie and others.

MELANIE—**f** 'Black-haired' (Greek).

MELANTHE, MELANTHA—**f** 'Dark flower' (Greek).

MELCHIOR—**m** 'King of light' (Hebrew). One of the Three Wise Men.

MELINDA—**f** Possibly a conflation of Melanie and Lucinda.

MELISSA—**f** 'Honey' or 'bee' (Greek). Legendary nymph who first taught the use of honey.

MELODY—**f** Used since the eighteenth century, but the reason for its first use is unknown.

MELVILLE—**m** Place-name/surname derivation.

MELVIN, MELVYN—**m** Place-name derivation but probably came from the USA.

MERCY—**f** A 'virtue' name arising in the seventeenth century.

MEREDITH—**f** An Old Welsh chief's name.

MERIEL—**f** Form of Muriel.

MERIT—**m** Recently introduced, perhaps hoping it would influence the baby's development into a worthy citizen.

MERLE—**f** Probably a contraction of Meriel. Merle Oberon (1911-79), famous film actress.

MERLIN—**m** The magician who supported the legendary King Arthur and made the famous Round Table.

MERRELL—**m** Of Welsh or Irish derivation, indicating 'son of Muriel'.

MERRY—**f** Straightforward use of the quality of cheerfulness. In Dickens's *Martin Chuzzlewit* Mr Pecksniff has daughters Mercy and Charity, known as Merry and Cherry.

MERVIN, MERVYN—**m** From Welsh Merfyn, of uncertain origin, now all over the English-speaking world. It might be from the place-name Myrddin, 'sea hill'.

MERYL—**f** Form of Muriel.

MIA—**f** (Scandinavian). Short form of Maria publicised through actress Mia Farrow (born 1945).

MICHAEL—**m** 'Who is like God' (Hebrew). One of the archangels, patron saint of the Crusaders.

MICHAELA—**f** Form of Michael.

MICHELLE—**f** French female form of Michael.

MIGNONETTE—**f** Victorian flower name.

MIKKI—**f** Affectionate form of Michaela, now used separately.

MILDRED—**f** 'Mild strength' (Old English). Victorian revival.

MILES—**m** Norman, possibly a pet form of Michael but also associated with Latin *miles,* 'soldier'.

MILLICENT, MELICENT—**f** 'Strength in labour' (Teutonic).

MILTON—**m** Place-name/surname derivation.

MIMI—**f** Affectionate short form of Miriam. Heroine of Puccini's opera *La Bohème* (1896).

MINA—**f** Short form of Wilhelmina.

MINNA—**f** May be linked to the medieval German notion of *Minne* or 'courtly love'. Introduction into England influenced by Sir Walter Scott's Minna Troil in *The Pirate* (1822).

MINNIE—**f** Pet-name for Jasmine, Wilhelmina or Mary, now quite independent.

MIRABEL—**f** 'Wonderful' (Latin).

MIRANDA—**f** 'Deserving admiration' (Latin). Appears to have been invented by Shakespeare for the heroine of *The Tempest.*

MIRELLA—**f** From a French name, Mireille, with the same basic origin as Miranda.

MIRIAM—**f** Of uncertain meaning; suggestions include 'the longed-for one' or 'star of the sea' (Hebrew). The Old Testament equivalent of Mary. The name of the sister of Moses and Aaron.

MITCHELL—**m** A form of Michael derived from a variant surname.

MO—**f** Short form of Maureen.

MODESTA—**f** Derived from Latin for 'decorous in manner and conduct'.

MOHAMMED—**m** 'Praiseworthy' (Muslim). Various spellings. After the prophet, *c.* 570-632, who founded the Islamic faith. By 1994 it had become 41st in the list of boys' names used in England and Wales.

MOHAN—**m** 'Most attractive' (Hindu).

MOIRA, MOYRA—**f** Irish variants of Mary, popular in Scotland.

MOLLY—**f** Pet-name for Mary. Rose up the chart of popularity through a small child named in a supermarket's television advertisement.

MONA—**f** Short form of Madonna; also may have a link with a Gaelic word for 'noble'. Name of an Irish saint which had a Victorian revival. 'Mona Lisa', famed portrait by Leonardo da Vinci.

MONICA—**f** 'Of good advice' (Latin). Origin uncertain. Saint who was mother of St Augustine. Popular in 1920s.

MONROE—**m** From Scottish surname Munro.

MONTAGUE—**m** Norman family name from Mont Aigu near Caen.

MONTGOMERY—**m** Place-name/surname derivation.

MORA—**f** 'Sun' (Gaelic).

MORAG—**f** 'Great' (Gaelic).

MORDECAI—**m** 'Man of Marduk' (Babylonian). Used in the book of Esther.

MORGAN—**m** or **f** 'Sea dweller' (Welsh).

MORLEY—**m** Place-name/surname origin.

MORNA, MYRNA—**f** 'Beloved' (Irish Gaelic). Forms of the original Gaelic name Muirnie.

MORRIS—**m** A variant of Maurice.

MORTIMER—**m** From the place Mortemer in Normandy.

MORTON—**m** From the English place-name.

MORVYTH—**f** 'Chieftainess' (Welsh).

MORWENNA—**f** 'Like a wave of the sea' (Welsh).

MOSES—**m** Thought to be linked to Egyptian names like Ramses and Tuthmosis, the name may mean 'born of [the water]', describing the discovery of the child Moses (the great leader of the Israelites) by an Egyptian princess.

MOSTYN—**m** 'Fortress' (Welsh).

MUNGO—**m** 'Lovable' (Gaelic). Mungo Park (1771-1806), explorer of the Niger in West Africa.

MURDOCH—**m** 'Mariner' or 'master' (Gaelic). Rare now as a forename.

MURIEL—**f** 'Seabright' (Celtic). Another authority says it denoted 'myrrh' in Arabic.

MURRAY—**m** 'Man of the sea' (Celtic). A well-known Scottish family name.

MUSIDORA—**f** 'Gift of the Muses' (Greek).

MYFANWY—**f** 'My fine one' (Welsh). Medieval use revived in Wales in nineteenth century. Title of a popular song sung by Welsh choirs.

MYRA—**f** Said to have been invented by Fulke Greville as the subject of his love poems.

MYRON—**m** 'Aromatic oil' (Greek). Myron was reputedly a Greek sculptor of miraculous talent.

MYRTLE—**f** One of the popular Victorian plant names.

NABEEL, NABEELA—**m** and **f** 'Noble, respected' (Muslim).

NADIA—**f** 'Hope' (Russian). Wife of Lenin.

NADINE—**f** A French form of Nadia.

NALANI—**f** 'Calmness of the heavens' (Hawaiian).

NANAK—**m** One of the names of the founder of Sikhism, who lived 1469-1539.

NANCY—**f** Diminutive of Anne.

NANETTE—**f** Elaboration of Ann with French diminutive ending. *No, No Nanette* (1925) was a popular musical by Vincent Youmans and Irving Caesar.

NAOMI—**f** 'Pleasure' (Hebrew). The mother-in-law of Ruth.

NARELLE—**f** A recent Australian introduction, possibly from the commercial name of a perfume.

NARMADA—**f** 'Gives pleasure' (Hindi).

NATALIE—**f** 'Christmas child' (Latin). French version of the original Latin, often used for girls born on Christmas Day.

NATASHA—**f** Russian version of Natalie.

NATHAN—**m** 'Gift' (Hebrew). More widely used in the USA. Hebrew prophet in the time of David.

NATHANIEL—**m** 'Gift of God' (Hebrew). One of Christ's disciples, better known as Bartholomew.

NAYANA—**f** 'Beautiful eyes' (Hindu).

NEIL—**m** Anglicised form of Niall.

NELIA—**f** Affectionate shortening of Cornelia.

NELLY—**f** Pet-form of Eleanor, Ellen or Helen.

NELSON—**m** From surname of famous British admiral Horatio Nelson (1758-1805). Given renewed circulation today as name of a character in the BBC radio serial *The Archers*.

NERISSA—**f** A Latin elaboration of the Greek for 'sea-nymph', first used by Shakespeare in *The Merchant of Venice.*

NERYS—**f** (Welsh) Origin uncertain. Now popular with the Welsh cultural revival.

NESTA—**f** Post-Conquest Welsh form of Agnes.

NETTA—**f** Diminutive of Janet.

NEVA—**f** 'Snow' (Latin), probably derived via Spanish *nieve* or Portugese *neve.* For a child born on a snowy day.

NEVILLE—**m** From the place Neuville in Normandy. Neville Chamberlain, British Prime Minister 1937-40.

NEWMAN—**m** (English). Surname derivation, mostly from the mother's maiden name.

NEWTON—**m** (English). Place-name/surname derivation. Often mother's maiden name used as forename.

NGAIO—**f** (New Zealand). From Maori for a 'timber tree'.

NIALL, NIAILL—**m** 'Champion' or 'passionate' (Gaelic). Used in Ireland, Scotland and Wales, the name also gave rise to the Nordic Njál as in *Njál's Saga.*

NIAZ—**m** 'Gift' (Hindu, from Persian).

NICHOLAS—**m** 'Victor for the people' (Greek). St Nicholas, fourth-century patron saint of children (as Santa Claus), sailors, pawnbrokers and thieves! Name of five popes, and of Nicholas Brakespeare, the only Englishman so appointed (as Adrian IV).

NICKI, NIKKI—**f** Short forms of Nicola, now used independently.

NICOLA, NICOLETTE—**f** Italian and French forms of Nicholas.

NIGEL—**m** Derived from Neil via the medieval Latin Nigellus (a diminutive of the Latin for 'black' or 'dark'.

NIMROD—**m** 'Valiant' (Hebrew).

NINA—**f** Russian diminutive of Anne.

NINIAN—**m** Corrupted form of Vivian.

NITA—**f** Short form of the Spanish Juanita, which could be translated as Joanie.

NOAH—**m** The biblical context (Genesis 5:29) suggests a meaning of 'rest' (Hebrew). Noah built the ark and saved all species of animals from the Flood.

NOEL—**m** or **f** 'Christmas child' (Old French). For children born on Christmas Day.

NOELEEN—**f** Came from Australia as Nolene in the 1960s. Noeline is a variant.

NOLA—**f** From Irish Nolan or a short form of Fenella. It is also the name of a place near Naples.

NOOR—**f** 'Holy light', to be read as 'light of my life' (Muslim).

NORA, NORAH—**f** An Irish or Scottish short form of Eleanor, Honor or Honora, now used independently.

NORBERT—**m** 'Famed in the north' (Teutonic).

NOREEN—**f** Irish diminutive of Nora.

NORMA—**f** 'Pattern' (Latin). Probably originates, in modern use, from Bellini's opera of that name, first performed 1851.

NORMAN—**m** 'Northman' (Old English).

NORRIS—**m** 'From the north' (Old French). A surname offshoot.

NUALA—**f** Affectionate form of Irish Fionnuala, 'white shoulders'.

OBADIAH—**m** 'Serving God' (Hebrew). Hebrew prophet.

OBERON—**m** Alternative spelling of Auberon. King of the fairies in Shakespeare's *A Midsummer Night's Dream*.

OCEAN—**m** or **f** Used for children born at sea, going back to Oceanus Hopkins, baptised on the historic voyage of the

Mayflower in 1620.

OCTAVIA—**f** 'Eighth child' (Latin). Also used for those born on the eighth day of the month.

ODETTE—**f** French diminutive variant of Odo or Otto. Odette Churchill was the British agent who survived Ravensbrück concentration camp in the Second World War.

ODILE—**f** French diminutive variant of Odo or Otto. Patron saint of Alsace, founded a convent at Odilienburg.

ODO—**m** Norman variant of Otto, rarely used. Odo, Bishop of Bayeux (*c.*1036-97), commissioned the Bayeux Tapestry.

OLGA—**f** Russian variant of Helga. Much used in vintage spy stories.

OLIVE, OLIVIA—**f** 'Olive' (Latin). Olivia is a character in Shakespeare's *Twelfth Night*.

OLIVER—**m** 'Olive tree' (Old French). Oliver Cromwell (1599-1658), Lord Protector of the Realm. Oliver Goldsmith, author of *The Vicar of Wakefield* (1760).

OLIVIA—**f** See Olive.

OLWEN—**m** or **f** 'Blessed footprints' (Welsh). White clover sprang up wherever the legendary heroine Olwen had walked. The name's recent popularity stems from the music *The Dream of Olwen*.

OMAR—**m** 'The highest' (Arabic) or 'eloquent' (Hebrew). Mentioned in the pedigree in Genesis 36:11. Omar Sharif (born 1926), film actor.

ONDINE—**f** Derived from Latin *unda*, 'wave'.

OPAL—**f** One of the Victorian borrowings from precious stones. Opaline is a variant.

OPHELIA—**f** 'Succour' (Greek). Invented by Sannazaro in his *Arcadia* (1504) and perpetuated by Shakespeare in *Hamlet*.

OPHRAH, OPHRA, OFRA—**m** or **f** 'Fawn' (Hebrew). A man's name in the Old Testament but now largely reserved for girls. Oprah Winfrey, American television personality.

ORALIE—**f** Recent invention, perhaps from French Aurélie.

ORIANA—**f** Perhaps from Latin *oriens,* 'dawning'. The name first appeared in a medieval French romance. Poets used it in referring to Queen Elizabeth I. Tennyson's 'Ballad of Oriana' brought it back to notice.

ORLANDO—**m** Italian form of Roland. Orlando Gibbons (1583-1625), English composer. Popularised by Virginia Woolf's novel *Orlando,* in which the main character changes sex.

ORNETTA—**f** Used in English today as a derivative from Ornella, a character in Gabriele d'Annunzio's *The Daughter of Jorio* (1906).

ORSON—**m** From a Norman nickname based on Latin *ursus,* 'bear'. Modern use may be due to Orson Welles (1915-85), American actor and film director.

ORVILLE—**m** French place-name ('gold town'). One of the Wright brothers, the first men to achieve powered flight (1903).

OSBERT—**m** 'God-bright' (Old English). The name refers to a pagan god rather than the Christian one. Osbert Sitwell (1892-1969), one of a famous family of writers.

OSBORN—**m** 'God-like man' (Old English).

OSCAR—**m** 'Spear of the gods' (Old English). Two kings of Sweden. Oscar Wilde (1856-1900), Irish writer of great wit.

OSMOND, OSMUND—**m** 'God's protection' (Old English), referring to a pagan god.

OSWALD—**m** 'Divinely powerful' (Old English). St Oswald (605-42) was king of Northumbria, and another saint of this name (died 992) was Archbishop of York.

OSWIN—**m** 'God's friend' (Old English), referring to a pagan god.

OTIS—**m** 'Keen of hearing' (Greek).

OTTO—**m** 'Riches' (Teutonic). Line of emperors of the Holy Roman Empire. Otto Klemperer (1885-1973), German conductor.

OWEN—**m** Probably a Celtic variant of Eugene, 'well-born'. A very popular Welsh name.

PADDY—**m** Short form of Patrick.

PALOMA—**f** 'Dove' (Spanish).

PAMELA—**f** Invented by Sir Philip Sidney for a character in his *Arcadia* (1590) and used by Richardson for his famous novel *Pamela* (1740).

PANSY—**f** Flower name.

PARIS—**m** In Greek legend the man who eloped with Helen of Troy and set off the Trojan Wars. Has been used to mark a baby's conception on honeymoon in Paris. Most popular in the USA.

PARKER—**m** 'Park keeper' (Old French). English surname sometimes used as a forename.

PARTHENOPE—**f** 'In the form of a maiden' (Greek). Pronounced as four syllables. One of the three Sirens of Greek legend, along with Ligea and Leucosia. The damsel loved by Prince Volscius in the Duke of Buckingham's *The Rehearsal* of 1731.

PASCAL—**m** 'Easter baby' (French). Refers to date of birth.

PATIENCE—**f** Seventeenth-century 'abstract quality' name.

PATRICE—**m** or **f** French form of Patrick. Actress Patrice Wymore is an example of its popularity in the USA.

PATRICIA—**f** Form of Patrick.

PATRICK—**m** 'Nobleman' (Latin). The name taken by the Celt Sucat (died *c*.468), when appointed missionary to Ireland.

PATTY—**f** Affectionate form of Patricia.

PAUL—**m** 'Small' (Greek). Saul took this name upon conversion to Christianity. The name of six popes.

PAULA—**f** Form of Paul.

PAULETTE—**f** A French diminutive form of Paula.

PAULINE—**f** A French form of Paula.

PEARL—**f** A modern gem name.

PEDRO—**m** Spanish form of Peter.

PEGGY—**f** Pet-form of Margaret.

PELHAM—**m** Place-name/surname derivation.

PELLA—**f** Swedish short form of Petronella.

PENELOPE—**f** Uncertain derivation, perhaps connected with the Greek word *pene*, 'bobbin'. In Greek mythology Penelope sat weaving while her husband Odysseus was away, and she renounced all suitors.

PENNY—**f** Affectionate form of Penelope now used in its own right.

PENROSE—**m** English place-name.

PENTHEA—**f** 'Fifth child' (Greek).

PEONY—**f** Flower name.

PEPITA—**f** A Spanish diminutive form of Josefina, but long used in English as a separate name.

PERCIVAL—**m** The great family name from Percheval in Normandy.

PERCY—**m** Short for Percival but used in its own right as a separate name from the great Norman family.

PERDITA—**f** 'Lost' (Latin). A Shakespearean invention for the heroine of *A Winter's Tale*.

PEREGRINE—**m** 'Traveller' (Latin). *The Adventures of Peregrine Pickle* by Tobias Smollett (1751).

PERNILLA—**f** Swedish form of Petronilla.

PERONELLE, PERONEL, PERNEL—**f** All forms of Petronella which go back to the middle ages.

PERRY—**m** 'Pear tree' (Old English). Originally from surname but given impetus by Erle Stanley Gardner's hero Perry Mason in many detective stories from 1933, later televised. May also be a short form of Peregrine.

PERSEPHONE—**f** (Greek). A beautiful goddess of Greek legend carried off by Pluto to be queen of the underworld. For this reason she is associated with death.

PETA—**f** A form of Peter.

PETAL—**f** Modern flower name.

PETER—**m** 'Rock' (Greek). One of the commonest forenames in every country. Given by Jesus to Simon, one of His three most favoured disciples.

PETRA—**f** Form of Peter.

PETRONELLA, PETRONILLA—**f** Diminutives of the Roman family name Petronius. Petronilla was a first-century martyr.

PETULA—**f** 'Saucy' (Latin). Petula Clark, singer.

PETUNIA—**f** 'Tobacco' (Tupi, language of South American Indian tribe). We know it as the name of a colourful flower for pots, bedding and window boxes.

PHELIM—**m** Irish form of old Gaelic Feidhlim, sixth-century disciple of St Columba.

PHILADELPHIA—**f** 'Ford of brother/sister' (Greek). Name of a city in the Bible which inspired William Penn when founding the American city. Used now in its short forms Delphia, Delphi.

PHILANDER—**m** 'Lover of his fellow man' (Greek).

PHILIP—**m** 'Lover of horses' (Greek). Philip of Macedon was father of Alexander the Great. One of the twelve apostles. Six kings of France and five of Spain.

PHILIPPA—**f** Form of Philip. Sometimes abbreviated to Pippa as in Browning's *Pippa Passes* (1841).

PHILLIDA—**f** Variant of Phyllis, also spelt Phyllida.

PHILOMENA—**f** A character in Greek mythology who was changed into a nightingale, giving her name to the bird.

PHINEAS—**m** 'The negro' (Egyptian). Phineas Fogg, central character in Jules Verne's *Around the World in Eighty Days* (1873).

PHOEBE—**f** 'Bright' (Greek). The Greek moon goddess. Also another name for Diana.

PHYLLIS—**f** 'Leafy' (Greek). The subject of Greek and Roman pastoral poetry, a legendary girl who hanged herself for love and was changed into an almond tree.

PIA—**f** 'Devout' (Latin).

PIERCE—**m** From surname derived from the forename Piers. Variants are Pearce and Pearson.

PIERS—**m** A French form of Peter but introduced so early that Langland wrote his *Piers Plowman* in the fourteenth century.

PIPPA—**f** Short form of Philippa.

PLATO—**m** 'Broad' (Greek). Nickname of the Greek philosopher whose real name was Aristocles.

PLEASANT—**f** 'Pleasing' or 'giving pleasure', in reference to the baby's birth. Name of character in Dickens's *Our Mutual Friend*. Pleasance and Pleasence are also used.

PLUSHA—**f** Used for a baby born in 1997. Uncertain derivation, probably from Latin *pilus,* 'hair', and so 'plushy' – a baby born with a good head of hair.

POLLY—**f** Diminutive of Mary or Paula.

POLLYANNA—**f** Largely due to popularity of Eleanor H. Porter's children's book *Pollyanna* (1913).

POPPY—**f** English flower name.

PORTIA—**f** From the Latin family name Porcius, 'pig farmer'. Unfortunate origin of a pleasant-sounding name used by Shakespeare for the heroine in *The Merchant of Venice*.

POSY—**f** Victorian flower name but also a possible children's short form of Josephine – Josy-Posy.

PRABHAT—**m** 'Dawn' (Hindu), remembering time of birth.

PRESCOTT—**m** Old English surname derivation.

PRESTON—**m** Place-name/surname derivation.

PRIMO—**m** 'First born' (Latin).

PRIMROSE—**f** Victorian flower name.

PRISCILLA—**f** 'Ancient' (Latin). From the Roman family name of Priscus.

PROSERPINA, PROSERPINE—**f** A Roman goddess. The daughter of Ceres and Jupiter, called Persephone by the Greeks. As queen of the underworld, she became associated with death. She is illustrated in one of Rossetti's most popular paintings.

PROSPER, PROSPERO—**m** 'Fortunate' (Latin).

PRUDENCE—**f** A 'virtue' name, meaning 'good sense'. Used as early as 348 for St Prudentius, one of the earliest hymn-writers of the Christian church.

PRUNELLA—**f** 'Little plum' (Latin).

QABIL—**m** 'Able, clever' (Muslim).

QUADIRA—**f** 'Powerful' (Muslim). Also used for boys sometimes.

QUEENIE—**f** Derived from Old English *Cwen,* 'woman', and popular in the nineteenth century, sometimes as a nickname for Victoria.

QUENTIN, QUINTIN—**m** 'Fifth' (Latin), used to denote a fifth child. *Quentin Durward* (1823), a novel by Sir Walter Scott.

QUIANA—**f** An invented name based on Anna, which has gained favour more in the USA than elsewhere. Short form is Kia.

QUINCY—**m** From a Norman surname and place-name, from the same root as Quentin. John Quincy Adams (1767-1848), sixth

President of the USA, was born at Quincy, Massachusetts.

QUINELLA, QUINETTA—**f** Forms of Quintin used in the USA.

QUINN—**m** 'Wise counsel' (Irish).

QUINTIN—**m** See under Quentin. Quintin Hogg (1845-1903), educationist and philanthropist.

RAB, RABBIE—**m** Scottish diminutive of Robert. 'Rabbie' Burns (1759-96), great Scottish poet.

RACHEL—**f** 'Ewe' (Hebrew). Younger sister of Leah and second and favourite wife of Jacob (Genesis 29-31).

RACHID, RACHIDA—**m** or **f** 'Wise' (Muslim). *Ar-rashid*, 'the guide', is one of the many names for Allah.

RADCLIFFE—**m** Taken from the surname arising from the place-name, meaning 'the red cliff'.

RADEGUND—**m** 'Wise in battle' (the name of several saints).

RADFORD—**m** Recent adoption of the surname.

RADHA—**f** 'Success' (Hindu).

RAE—**f** Short form of Rachel.

RAELENE—**f** Typical Australian elaboration of Rae.

RALEIGH—**m** Place-name/surname derivation. Sir Walter Raleigh (1552-1618), sailor and adventurer, started colonisation of Virginia in 1584.

RALPH—**m** Contraction of Randolph. *Ralph Roister Doister* (*c*.1540) is the earliest known English comedy.

RAMONO—**f** Form of the Spanish version of Raymond.

RAMSAY—**m** Place-name/surname derivation. Inspiration for use from James Ramsay Macdonald, Labour politician, Prime Minister 1924 and 1929-31.

RANDAL—**m** A medieval form of Randolph.

RANDOLPH—**m** 'Shield-wolf' (Old English). Also a Norman name that evolved from Old Norse.

RANJANA—**f** 'Adorable' (Hindu).

RANULF—**m** A medieval form of Randolph.

RAOUL—**m** French form of Ralph. Raoul Dufy (1877-1953), painter.

RAPHAEL—**m** 'Whom God has healed' (Hebrew). One of the seven archangels, the angel of healing. Raphael (1483-1520),

Italian painter.

RAQUEL—**f** Spanish form of Rachel. Made popular through glamorous film actress Raquel Welch, born in Chicago in 1940.

RAVI—**m** 'Sun' (Sanskrit). Hindu god of the sun.

RAY—**m** or **f** Short form of Raymond or Rachel.

RAYMOND—**m** 'Wise protector' (Teutonic). Shortened to Ray.

RAYNA—**f** Started in USA around 1940 as a feminine form of Ray and spawned variants Rayann, Rayetta, Rainell.

RAYNER—**m** From a Norman surname, derived from the Teutonic for 'adviser of armies'.

REA—**f** Affectionate diminutive of Andrea.

REANNA—**f** Modern invented name perhaps from Welsh Rhiannon.

REBECCA—**f** Of uncertain Aramaic derivation. Wife of Isaac and sister of Laban.

REDWALD—**m** 'Powerful adviser' (Old English).

REES—**m** Surname derivation from the Welsh Rhys.

REGAN—**f** One of the three daughters of King Lear in Shakespeare's play.

REGINA—**f** 'Queen' (Latin).

REGINALD—**m** A Norman Latinised form of Reynold.

RÉMY, REMUS—**m** 'Oarsman', developed from Latin through French influence.

RENA—**f** Recent introduction based on Renée.

RENATA—**f** 'Born again' (Latin). Renata Tebaldi, Italian opera singer (born 1922).

RENÉ—**m** 'Born again'. French version of Renata.

RENÉE—**f** Feminine form of René.

RESEDA—**f** 'Mignonette' (Latin). A flower name.

REUBEN—**m** 'Behold a son' (Hebrew). One of the sons of Jacob, and the progenitor of a tribe of Israel.

REX—**m** 'King' (Latin). An innovation of the twentieth century. Rex Whistler (1905-44), English artist.

REYNARD—**m** 'Decisive and strong' (Teutonic), introduced by the Normans. Reynard the Fox is the subject of a German epic.

REYNOLD—**m** 'Decisive ruler' (Teutonic), introduced by the Normans. Gave rise to surnames from earliest times.

RHEA—**f** In Roman legend, the mother of Romulus and Remus, the founders of Rome itself. Has been extended recently to Rheanna.

RHETT—**m** Invented for character Rhett Butler in Margaret Mitchell's *Gone with the Wind* (1936).

RHIAN, RHIANNON—**f** 'Maiden' (Welsh). True Welsh form is Rhiain. Used as a forename only since the 1940s.

RHODA—**f** 'Rose' (Greek). First mentioned in Acts 12:13.

RHONA, RONA—**f** Modern invention, started in Scotland in Victorian times, possibly from the island in the Hebrides.

RHONWEN—**m** 'Tall and slender' (Welsh).

RHYS—**m** 'Ardour' (Welsh). Various Welsh tribal leaders of the pre-Conquest period.

RICHARD—**m** 'Tough ruler' (Old English). One of the most popular men's names throughout history with many diminutives and nicknames, like Dick, Dickie, Rick.

RICHIE—**m** Scottish and Australian diminutive of Richard. Richie Benaud (born 1930), Australian cricketer then commentator.

RICHMAL—**f** Probably a blend of Richard and Mary. The name was first borne by Richmal Crompton (1890-1969), author of *Just William* books.

RICKY—**m** Short form of Richard now used in its own right. Has given rise to feminine form of Rikki.

RIJU—**f** 'Pure and innocent' (Hindu).

RITA—**f** Short form of Margaret originating in Italy.

ROALD—**m** 'Fame and power' (Old Norse). Made famous by Roald Amundsen (1872-1928), the Norwegian who beat Captain Scott to the South Pole in December 1911. The popularity of the children's books of Roald Dahl (1916-90) has assured its use through another generation.

ROBERT—**m** 'Shining fame' (Old English). A very popular name from the beginning of the English language. Robert the Bruce, king of Scotland 1306-29.

ROBERTA—**f** Form of Robert.

ROBIN—**m** or **f** A diminutive of Robert from earliest times, as in Robin Hood, Robin Goodfellow.

ROBINA—**f** Form of Robin.

ROBYN—**f** Form of Robin used largely in the USA.

ROCCO—**m** Italian form of a German name of the middle ages.

ROCK—**m** 'Peter' in modern language.

RODERICA—**f** Form of Roderick.

RODERICK—**m** 'Famous ruler' (Teutonic). *Roderick Random* (1748), a novel by Tobias Smollett.

RODNEY—**m** 'Isle among the reeds' (Old English). Originally from Rodney Stoke, the village in Somerset which produced the surname. Its use as a forename boosted by Lord Rodney (1719-92), the admiral.

ROGER—**m** 'Famous with the spear' (Old English/Teutonic). The Norman Roger I (1031-1101) ruled Sicily.

ROISIN—**f** (Irish). Diminutive of Rois, English Rosa, flower name from the nineteenth century.

ROLAND, ROWLAND—**m** 'Famous throughout the land' (Teutonic). One of Charlemagne's lords, subject of the *Chanson de Roland*, a medieval French romance.

ROLF—**m** Contraction of Rudolph.

ROLLO—**m** Affectionate shortening of Roland.

ROMAINE—**f** Recent English introduction from the French for a woman born in Rome.

ROMOLA—**f** 'Woman of Rome' (Latin).

RONA—**f** Hebridean place-name.

RONALD—**m** Scottish form of Reynold.

RONAN—**m** From the Gaelic, which can be roughly translated as 'little seal'.

RORY—**m** 'Red' (Gaelic).

ROSA—**f** 'Rose' (Latin). St Rosa (1556-1617) has her feast-day on 31st August.

ROSALIE—**f** 'Rosalia', the Romans' yearly custom of decorating tombs with roses (Latin). Twelfth-century saint of Palermo noted for her extreme penitence.

ROSALIND—**f** 'Horse-serpent', i.e. 'dragon' (Teutonic). Later reinterpreted as *rosa linda*, 'pretty rose' (Spanish), which is its modern connotation. Popular through the character in Shakespeare's *As You Like It*.

ROSAMUND—**f** 'Protector of horses' (Teutonic). A fifth-century Hrosmund was compelled by her husband to drink his health in a goblet formed of her murdered father's skull! Rosamund Clifford, 'Fair Rosamund', mistress of Henry II, died *c.*1176.

ROSANNE, ROSEANN—**f** Modern combination of Rose and Anne.

ROSCOE—**m** From the surname.

ROSE—**f** A flower name used from the very beginning of personal names, giving rise to a common surname and the old joke: 'Rose Rose sat on a pin—Rose Rose rose!'

ROSEMARY—**f** 'Sea dew' (Latin), but popular as a plant name from Victorian times.

ROSETTA—**f** Form of Rose. Town in North Africa where the Rosetta Stone was found (1799), which was the key to the deciphering of Egyptian hieroglyphs.

ROSHEEN—**f** Introduced around 1960 as a phonetic spelling of Roisin.

ROSS—**m** 'Horse' (Old Norse), or 'headland' (Celtic). Mainly Scottish name derived from a surname/place-name.

ROWENA—**f** 'Famous friend' (Old English). The Saxon heroine of Scott's *Ivanhoe* (1820).

ROWLAND—**m** See under Roland.

ROXANNE—**f** 'Dawn' (Persian). Roxana was the wife of Alexander the Great.

ROY—**m** 'Red' (Gaelic). But users of the name today usually have in mind the French *roi*, king.

ROYSTON—**m** Place-name/surname derivation from the place in Hertfordshire.

ROZELLA—**f** Modern diminutive of Rose.

RUBY—**f** One of the modern 'precious stone' names.

RUCHIKA—**f** 'Lovely' (Hindu).

RUDOLF, RUDOLPH—**m** 'Famous wolf' (Teutonic). Its popularity was increased by the fame of Rudolf Valentino (1895-1926), heart-throb of early American films.

RUDYARD—**m** English place-name made famous by the poet Rudyard Kipling (1865-1936).

RUFUS—**m** 'Red-haired' (Latin). William Rufus (William II), king of England 1087-1100, was killed while hunting in the New Forest. The Rufus Stone marks the spot.

RUPERT—**m** Form of Robert. Introduced to England by the popular Prince Rupprecht (1619-82), nephew of Charles I.

RUPINDER—**f** 'Most beautiful' (Hindu).

RUSSELL—**m** 'Little red-haired one' (French). Developed from nickname to surname and thence to forename.

RUTH—**f** Uncertain derivation, but the modern meaning of 'compassion' may influence its choice.

RYAN—**m** From the Irish Gaelic surname Ó Riain, perhaps originally from a root denoting royal status.

SABA—**f** (Hebrew). An alternative of Sheba, an area of Arabia mentioned in the Bible. Sidney Smith (1776-1845), the essayist, used it to name his eldest daughter.

SABELL—**f** Invented name, removing the first and last letters from Isabella.

SABIN, SABINA—**f** 'Of the Sabine race' (Latin).

SABRINA—**f** 'Severn' (Latin). The river.

SACHA—**m** French from Sasha, a Russian affectionate short form of Alexander. Sacha Distel, present-day French singer.

SADIE—**f** Diminutive of Sarah.

SAFFRON—**f** Flower name. A kind of crocus. Saffron Walden, an old town in Essex known for the flower grown there in millions to make the saffron used for dyeing, medicine and food.

SAFI, SAFIA—**m** and **f** 'My best friend' (Muslim).

SAJAN—**m** 'Beloved' (Hindu).

SALIM—**m** 'Safe, peaceful' (Muslim).

SALLIANNE—**f** A recent fanciful conjoining of Sally and Anne.

SALLY—**f** Pet-name for Sarah, now used independently.

SALOME—**f** 'Peaceful' (Aramaic). A Greek rendering. She procured the death of John the Baptist as a reward for her dancing before King Herod.

SAM—**m** or **f** A contraction, now used quite independently, of Samuel, Samantha, Sampson.

SAMANTHA—**f** Origin unknown, but could be a contraction of Samuel and Anthea or derived from Samandal, the undersea empire in the *Arabian Nights*.

SAMARIA—**f** A Black American name, either a development of Samantha, or from the region of Palestine mentioned in the Bible.

SAMINA—**f** 'Plump, chubby' (Muslim).

SAMPSON, SAMSON—**m** A Hebrew name, probably from the word *shemesh,* 'sun'. Samson was the strong man of the Bible (Book of Judges).

SAMUEL—**m** 'God has heard' or 'called by God' (Hebrew). Prophet following Moses and giving his name to the books of the Old Testament which tell his story.

SANCHIA—**f** Form of Sancho.

SANCHO—**m** A Spanish rendering of the Latin for 'holy'. Famous through Sancho Panza, Don Quixote's squire in Cervantes's novel (1615).

SANDIE—**f** An affectionate form of Sandra now used independently, perhaps influenced by Sandie Shaw, the bare-footed pop singer of the 1960s.

SANDRA—**f** Diminutive form of the Italian for Alexander, now quite separate.

SANDY—**m** or **f** Short form of Alexander and Alexandra, but also given as a separate name.

SANJAY—**m** 'Victorious' (Sanskrit). Sanjay Gandhi (1940-80) died in a plane crash.

SAPPHIRE—**f** Name of the precious stone.

SARAH, SARA—**f** 'Princess' (Hebrew). Sarah Siddons (1755-1831), foremost tragic actress of her time.

SASHA—**m** or **f** Anglicised Russian diminutive of Alexander or Alexandra.

SASKIA—**f** Origin unknown. Used since twelfth century, spreading throughout Europe.

SAUL—**m** 'The longed for' (Hebrew). The first king of Israel. Saul of Tarsus, when converted to Christianity, became St Paul.

SAYER—**m** Surname derivation, meaning 'sawyer' (medieval French), 'reciter' (Old English) or 'one who tests' (Middle English).

SCARLET—**f** From the colour. Scarlett O'Hara, heroine of *Gone with the Wind* by Margaret Mitchell, novel and film, 1939.

SCIPIO—**m** Family name of great Roman general, 237-183 BC.

SCHOLEM—**m** 'Peace' (Hebrew).

SCOTT—**m** A very early surname, obviously from Scotland. Used more in newer countries as a forename. F. Scott Fitzgerald (1896-1940), American novelist.

SEAMUS—**m** Irish form of James. Seamus Heaney (born 1939), poet.

SEAN—**m** Irish form of John which is gaining popularity, perhaps after Sean Connery (born 1930), film actor.

SEBASTIAN—**m** 'To be respected' (Greek). St Sebastian was a Christian Roman soldier martyred by being shot through with arrows. Sebastian Cabot (*c.*1475-1557), navigator and explorer.

SEBERT—**m** 'Famous in victory' (Teutonic).

SEFTON—**m** Place-name derivation.

SELENA, SELINA—**f** 'The moon' (Greek). A moon goddess.

SELIMA—**f** Origin unknown, but *selim* is Arabic for 'peace'. First used by Thomas Gray for Thomas Walpole's cat in his poem about its drowning 'in a tub of goldfishes'.

SELMA—**f** 'Fair' (Celtic), though another source says 'unfair'! May also be a variant of Anselm.

SELWYN—**m** 'Hall friend' (Old English), in other words a companion or colleague. Derives from the surname.

SERAPHINA—**f** 'Angelic' (Hebrew).

SERENA—**f** 'Calm' (Latin).

SERGE—**m** French form of Russian Sergei, an old family name.

SETH—**m** 'Consolation' (Hebrew). More common now in the USA.

SEYMOUR—**m** From a French place-name.

SHALOM—**m** 'Peace' (Hebrew).

SHAMUS—**m** Another spelling of Seamus.

SHAN—**f** An English phonetic rendering of the Welsh Sian that has grown in popularity since the mid 1950s.

SHANE—**m** English rendering of the Irish Sean.

SHANEE—**f** Anglicised Welsh form of Jane.

SHANKARA—**m** 'Lucky charm' (Hindu). Shankaracharya (AD 788-820), influential Hindu religious leader.

SHARON—**f** 'A plain' (Hebrew).

SHASH—**f** 'Moonbeam' (Hindu). One of the queens of Chauhan king Prithviraja (1162-92).

SHAUN, SHAWN—**m** Anglicised spellings of Sean.

SHAW—**m** Geographical ('wood' or 'copse'), then surname

derivation.

SHEELA—**f** 'Kind' (Hindu).

SHEENA, SHEENAGH—**f** Irish Gaelic form of Jane.

SHEILA, SHELAGH—**f** Gaelic forms of Cecilia or Celia, but now quite separate.

SHELLEY—**f** From the surname.

SHERIDAN—**m** Surname origin.

SHERLOCK—**m** 'With short hair' (Old English). Closely identified with Conan Doyle's detective Sherlock Holmes, who first appeared in the *Strand Magazine* in 1891.

SHERRY—**f** Anglicised form of French *chérie*, 'darling'.

SHEVAUN—**f** A modern spelling of the Gaelic Siobhan.

SHIREEN, SHIRIN—**f** A modern name based on old Persian or Arabic whose meaning is unknown.

SHIRLEY—**f** Place-name/surname derivation. Charlotte Brontë's *Shirley* (1849) is believed to have set the fashion.

SHOLTO—**m** A Scottish name derived from a Gaelic name meaning 'sower'. Sir William Sholto Douglas (1893-1969), fighter pilot who became a wartime leader of the RAF.

SHONA—**f** A Gaelic form of Jane.

SHONA—**f** 'Red' (Hindu), a name for a red-haired baby.

SHULA—**f** (Hebrew). A short form of Shulamite. Its use has spread through a character in the radio serial *The Archers*.

SIAN—**f** A Welsh variant of Jane.

SIBYL—**f** 'Wise woman' (Greek). In classical times a mouthpiece of the oracle. Disraeli's novel *Sybil* (1845) may have led to its revival.

SIDNEY—**m** 'St Denis' (French). Place-name in Anjou which identifies the great family of which Sir Philip Sidney was a member.

SIDONIE—**f** 'From Sidon' (Latin).

SIEGFRIED—**m** 'Victory and peace' (Teutonic). Hero of the German saga, the *Nibelungenlied*. Publicised by a character in the television series *All Creatures Great and Small*.

SIGMUND—**m** 'Victorious protector' (Teutonic).

SIGRID—**f** 'Victorious fair one' (Teutonic).

SILAS—**m** Short form of Silvanus, the Roman god of the forest, or of Sylvester. *Silas Marner* by George Eliot (1861).

SILVESTER—**m** Variant spelling of Sylvester. St Silvester is said to have cured the Emperor Constantine of leprosy.

SIMEON—**m** 'Listening' (Hebrew). Old Testament name which in the New Testament is always rendered as Simon. One of the twelve sons of Jacob. St Simeon Stylites (died 459) spent the last thirty years of his life on an 18 metre high pillar.

SIMON—**m** New Testament form of Simeon, which may also

reflect the Greek term for 'snub-nosed'. 'Simon, called Peter', one of the twelve apostles.

SIMONE—**f** Form of Simon.

SINCLAIR—**m** From 'St Clare', via the place-name.

SINDY—**f** Variant of Cindy sometimes used in USA.

SIOBHAN—**f** Irish Gaelic form of Jane.

SOHAN—**m** 'Handsome' (Hindu)

SOLANGE—**f** French variant of the Latin for 'solemn' in the religious sense. Name of a ninth-century saint who died resisting rape.

SOLOMON—**m** From the Hebrew *shalom,* 'peace'. Solomon, king of Israel, noted for his wisdom.

SOMERSET—**m** Rare use of the name of the county. W. Somerset Maugham (1874-1965), writer.

SONIA, SONYA—**f** Russian forms of Sophia. Sonya is the heroine of Dostoyevsky's *Crime and Punishment.*

SOPHIA—**f** 'Wisdom' (Greek). Popular with German royal families in the eighteenth century.

SOPHIE—**f** Form of Sophia.

SPENCER—**m** Short form of 'dispenser', housekeeper in a noble household. Charles Spencer, second Duke of Marlborough, passed on his surname as a forename to Sir Winston Leonard Spencer Churchill. Spencer Perceval was the only British Prime Minister to be assassinated (1812).

SPERATA—**f** 'The hoped-for one' (Latin).

SPIKE—**m** Referring to baby's tuft of hair; sometimes a nickname in later life.

STACEY—**f** Also spelt Stacy, Stacie. Possibly short forms of Anastasia or Eustacia.

STANFORD—**m** From the place-name via the surname.

STANLEY—**m** 'Stony field' (Teutonic). Place-name derivation.

STAR—**f** Recent invention which replaces Stella, its Latin equivalent.

STEFFI—**f** Diminutive of Stephanie. Steffi Graf (born 1969), German tennis champion.

STELLA—**f** 'Star' (Latin). Modern use attributed to its use in literature by Sir Philip Sidney, Waller and Swift. Also popular with Roman Catholics in the context of 'Stella Maris', a Latin translation of Miriam (Mary).

STEPHANIE—**f** Form of Stephen.

STEPHEN, STEVEN—**m** 'Crown' (Greek). St Stephen was the first Christian martyr. Five kings of Hungary and several popes have borne this name.

STUART, STEWART—**m** 'Guardian of the hall' (Old English), as in the more recent word 'steward'. Scottish royal family name.

The Stuart dynasty came to England with the accession of James VI of Scotland as James I of England.

SUKIE—**f** Diminutive of Susan. Used more in the eighteenth century than now. Enshrined in the nursery rhyme: 'Polly put the kettle on … Sukie take it off again …'

SUMAN—**m** 'Clever and wise' (Hindu).

SUMPTA—**f** Contraction of 'assumption' – the taking of the Virgin Mary in bodily form into heaven. The festival celebrated on 15th August makes it popular for baby girls born on that day.

SUNAYANA—**f** 'Beautiful eyes' (Hindu).

SUSAN—**f** English form of Susannah.

SUSANNA, SUSANNAH—**f** 'Lily' (Hebrew). Wife of Joachim, the subject of *The History of Susanna*, one of the books of the Apocrypha.

SUZANNE—**f** French form of Susannah.

SUZETTE—**f** Modern French diminutive of Susannah.

SWITHIN, SWITHUN—**m** 'Strong' (Old English). St Swithun (died 852) was Bishop of Winchester.

SYBIL—**f** Alternative spelling of Sibyl.

SYDEL—**f** 'Enchantress' (Hebrew).

SYDNEY—**m** Very common variant of Sidney, obviously associated with the capital city of New South Wales, Australia.

SYLVESTER—**m** 'Of the woods' (Latin). This was the name of a line of popes down to the twelfth centruy. Sylvester Stallone, actor.

SYLVIA—**f** 'Wood nymph' (Latin). Sometimes Silvia. Rhea Silvia was mother, by Mars, of Romulus and Remus, founders of Rome.

SYON—**m** 'Happy and beautiful' (Hindu).

TABITHA—**f** 'Doe' (Aramaic). The dead woman restored to life by St Peter (Acts 9: 36—41). Its Greek equivalent is Dorcas.

TAD—**m** Short form of Thaddeus now used separately, mostly in USA.

TALBOT—**m** 'Woodcutter' (French). Based on the surname of the Earls of Shrewsbury.

TALIA—**f** 'Blooming' (Greek). Spelt 'Thalia' as from the Latin when used in 1906.

TALIESIN—**m** 'Of the radiant force' (Welsh).

TALLULAH—**f** Originated in USA, possibly from Indian place-name. Tallulah Bankhead (1903-68), American actress so named after her grandmother.

TAMAR, TAMARA—**f** 'Palm tree' (Hebrew).

TAMSIN—**f** A feminine form of Thomas.

TANCRED—**m** 'Thoughtful counsellor' (Teutonic). The king of Sicily who imprisoned Richard Coeur de Lion during the Third Crusade.

TANSY—**f** Plant name.

TANYA, TANIA—**f** Independent forms of Tatiana, the Russian name.

TARA—**f** English borrowing from Irish place-name. Interest revived in 1960s after character in television series *The Avengers*.

TARQUIN—**m** (Latin). Name of two kings of Rome in the sixth century BC.

TASHA—**f** Short form of Natasha now often used separately.

TEAL—**f** After the small duck.

TEDDY—**m** Form of Edward or Theodore used in its own right.

TEGEN—**f** 'Beautiful' (Welsh).

TEL—**m** Short form of Terence or Terry used in its own right since popularisation by a character in television series *Minder* in 1980s.

TERENCE—**m** Unknown meaning. A Roman family name (Terentius). Terence was a comic poet of the second century BC.

TERENTIA—**f** Form of Terence. Wife of Cicero.

TERESA, THERESA—**f** Origin obscure. May denote someone from the island of Thera (Santorini) or derive from Greek *theros,* 'harvest'. Established in the western world through St Teresa of Avila (1515-82), and revived by the fame of St Thérèse of Lisieux (1873-97).

TERRY—**m** or **f** Once a separate given name, now used more as a short form of Terence or Teresa.

TESSA—**f** Short form of Teresa.

THADDEUS—**m** 'Praising Jehovah' (Hebrew). Also a form of Theodore. One of the lesser of Christ's apostles. Derived from the ancient Greek.

THEA—**f** 'Goddess' (Greek).

THELMA—**f** From the novel *Thelma, A Norwegian Princess* (1887) by Marie Corelli, who, it seems, invented the name.

THEO—**m** Short form of Theodore or Theobald now used separately. Theo was the devoted brother of Vincent Van Gogh (1853-90).

THEOBALD—**m** 'One of the bold people' (Teutonic).

THEODORA—**f** Form of Theodore.

THEODORE—**m** 'God's gift' (Greek). St Theodore, Archbishop of Canterbury in the seventh century. Theodore Roosevelt, President of the USA 1901-9. In Wales takes the form of Tudor.

THEODORIC—**m** 'Ruler of the tribe' (Teutonic).

THEODOSIA—**f** Feminine form of Theodore.

THEOPHILUS—**m** 'Beloved of God' (Greek).

THERESA—**f** See Teresa.

THIRZA—**f** Possibly a Hebrew place-name originally. Shown as Tirza in the book of Numbers.

THOMAS—**m** 'Twin' (Aramaic). One of the apostles (Doubting Thomas). Thomas à Becket (1118-70), Archbishop of Canterbury murdered in his cathedral.

THOMASIN, THOMASINA—**f** Diminutive form of Thomas.

THORA—**f** 'Of Thor' (Teutonic). Thor was the god of thunder.

THURSTAN—**m** 'Thor's stone' (Old English).

THYRZA—**f** Relating to Tyr, the Scandinavian god of war.

TIFFANY—**f** From Greek Theophania, 'manifestation of God'. The modern version of the name was probably popularised by the American jewellers, Tiffany's.

TILLY—**f** Short form of Matilda.

TIMOTHY—**m** 'Honouring God' (Greek). St Paul's companion.

TINA—**f** Pet form of Christine.

TIPU—**m** 'Tiger' (Hindu). Tipu Sultan (1750-99), ruler of Mysore.

TITUS—**m** A Latin *praenomen* (forename) of which the meaning is lost.

TOBIAS—**m** From Tobiah, 'God is good' (Hebrew). The book of Tobit, whose son was Tobias, is part of the Apocrypha. Tobias Smollett (1721-71), early English novelist.

TOBY—**m** Form of Tobias.

TODD, TOD—**m** 'Fox' (Old English). From surname implying, in dialect, the cunning of the fox.

TONI—**f** An independent short form of Antonia popular in the USA.

TOPAZ—**f** A recent addition to the casket of jewel names.

TORY—**f** Independently used short form of Victoria.

TRACEY, TRACY—**f** Place-name/surname derivation. Its popularity from the 1960s may have been from Grace Kelly's role as Tracy Lord in the film *High Society* in 1956.

TRELAWNEY—**m** Place-name/surname origin.

TREVELYAN—**m** Place-name/surname derivation.

TREVOR—**m** From a surname/place-name meaning 'large settlement' (Welsh).

TRICIA—**f** Independent short form of Patricia.

TRINA—**f** Short form of Katrina. Also a Hindu name meaning 'blades of sacred Kusa grass'.

TRISTAN—**m** Form of Tristram derived from French *triste*, 'sad', a surname by the twelfth century. Wagner's *Tristan und Isolde*, first performed 1865, may be an influence in its choice, as may a character in the television series *All Creatures Great and Small*.

TRISTRAM—**m** 'Rumbustious' (Celtic). Mentioned in the tales of King Arthur. *Tristram Shandy* (1767) is a novel by Laurence Sterne.

TRIXIE—**f** Short form of Beatrix used as a separate name.

TRUDY—**f** Independent short form of Gertrude and other names ending in -trude.

TRYPHENA—**f** 'Dainty' (Greek). Daughters of two of the Ptolemys of Egypt.

TUDOR—**m** See Theodore.

TURLOUGH—**m** A common Irish name of indeterminate origin but often translating Terence or Charles.

UBIGUD—**m** Phonetic rendering of 'You be good', reflecting parents' hopes. A fanciful recent introduction.

ULLA—**f** 'Jewel of the sea' (Gaelic).

ULRIC—**m** 'Rich and powerful' (Teutonic).

ULTIMA—**f** 'Last' (Latin).

ULYSSES—**m** The Latin rendering of the Greek Odysseus, hero of the legend. Ulysses S. Grant, general in the American Civil War, was elected eighteenth President of the USA in 1868.

UNA—**f** 'One' (Latin). Also a variant of Agnes or Winifred.

UNDINE—**f** A water-sprite in Roman mythology.

UNITY—**f** An 'abstract quality' name. Unity Mitford (1914-48), sister of authoress Nancy Mitford, was a notorious Nazi sympathiser.

UPTON—**m** Place-name/surname derivation. Upton Beall Sinclair (1878-1968), American socialist novelist.

URBAN—**m** 'City dweller' (Latin). Several Popes adopted it, ruling as they did from the Vatican City.

URIAH—**m** 'God is light' (Hebrew). Husband of Bathsheba in the Bible. Any hope of its popularity was dashed by its use by Dickens for Uriah Heep in *David Copperfield*.

URSULA—**f** 'Little she-bear' (Latin). St Ursula was an early martyr.

USHMIL—**f** 'Affectionate' (Hindu).

VALDA—**f** 'Powerful' (Teutonic).

VALENCIA—**f** A Spanish place-name.

VALENE—**f** Recent Australian invention.

VALENTIA, VALENTINA—**f** Female forms of Valentine.

VALENTINE—**m** 'Strong' or 'courageous' (Latin). A Roman Christian martyr of the third century who gave his name to the previously pagan festival of lovers on 14th February. One of Shakespeare's *Two Gentlemen of Verona*.

VALERIAN—**m** Masculine form of Valerie – 'healthy'.

VALERIE—**f** Probably from Latin *valere*, 'to be healthy'.

VANCE—**m** Place-name/surname related to Fann ('fen').

VANDA—**f** Variant of Wanda reflecting German pronunciation.

VANESSA—**f** From Greek *phanessa*, 'butterfly'. Used by Jonathan Swift to represent Esther Vanhomrigh, the subject of his poems.

VAREN—**m** 'The best' (Hindu).

VASHTI—**f** 'Belt' (Persian).

VASILI—**m** A Russian form of Basil.

VAUGHAN—**m** A recent borrowing of the old family name. Ralph Vaughan Williams (1872-1958), English composer.

VEAREY—**f** An original diminutive of Vera.

VEDA, VIDA—**f** Affectionate form of Davida but used separately since the late nineteenth century. A Veda is also a sacred Hindu scripture.

VELMA—**f** Recent invention in USA possibly based on Thelma.

VENA, VINA—**f** Affectionate short form of a number of names like Davina, Elvina, Malvina.

VENETIA—**f** 'Of the Venetic people' (Latin). Also the region around Venice. Venetia Stanley, renowned seventeenth-century beauty.

VERA—**f** 'True' (Latin). Its popularity may have stemmed from the character of this name in *A Cigarette-Maker's Romance* (1890) by F. Marion Crawford.

VERE—**m** 'Ver' in Normandy identified the great de Vere family, who as Earls of Oxford had an important role in the affairs of England.

VERENA—**f** Swiss place-name, probably chosen simply for its pleasant sound. Also variant of Vera.

VERGIL—**m** Variant of Virgil, found mostly in USA.

VERITY—**f** An early 'abstract quality' name.

VERNA—**f** 'Born in the spring' (Latin).

VERNON—**m** A Norman place and family name.

VERONA—**f** Current from late Victorian times, perhaps from the name of the Italian city.

VERONICA—**f** Variant of Berenice. St Veronica is said to have offered Christ a cloth to wipe his face on the way to Calvary, and the cloth was imprinted with his image. Also a flower name, from the genus of plants.

VESTA—**f** Roman goddess of fire, attended by the famous Vestal Virgins. Vesta Tilley was a music-hall star.

VEVINA—**f** 'The sweet woman' (Gaelic).

VICTOR—**m** 'Conqueror' (Latin). Popular in England in the nineteenth century as a compliment to Queen Victoria.

VICTORIA—**f** 'Victory' (Latin). Queen Victoria (1819-1901), named after her German mother, set the fashion, which is reviving.

VINCENT—**m** 'Conquering' (Latin). St Vincent, martyred in Spain in 304.

VIOLA—**f** 'Violet' (Latin). Heroine of Shakespeare's *Twelfth Night*.

VIOLET—**f** A Victorian flower name.

VIOLETTA—**f** Diminutive of Violet. The heroine of Verdi's opera *La Traviata* (1853), based upon the play *La Dame aux Camélias* by Dumas the Younger.

VIRGIL—**m** From the great Roman poet Publius Vergilius Maro (70-19 BC).

VIRGINIA—**f** 'Virginal' (Latin). A Roman family name but later and perhaps of greater significance a reference to Elizabeth I, the Virgin Queen, after whom Virginia, the American settlement, was named in 1584.

VIVA—**f** 'Alive' (Latin). Inferring a lively, happy baby.

VIVIAN—**m** 'Lively' (Latin).

VIVIEN, VIVIENNE—**f** Variants of Vivian.

WALDO—**m** A short form of names containing the element *wald,* 'power'.

WALFORD—**m** Place-name/surname derivation. Henry Walford Davies (1869-1941). The Welsh composer was Master of the King's Musick.

WALLACE—**m** Scottish family name made popular by William Wallace (died 1305), who beat the English at the battle of Stirling Bridge (1297).

WALLIS—**m** or **f** Variant of Wallace most influenced in use by Bessie Wallis Warfield, Duchess of Windsor (1896-1986), who married the former Edward VIII after his abdication.

WALTER—**m** 'Military leader' (Teutonic). A favourite Norman name as shown in the great Fitzwalter family.

WANDA—**f** May have Teutonic roots denoting a member of the slavic tribe of Vandals. Ouida's *Wanda* (1883) may have started the fashion.

WARD—**m** 'Protector' (Teutonic). Element of many early names but deriving from the later common surname.

WARNER—**m** Place-name/surname derivation.

WARREN—**m** 'Game park' (Middle English). Warren Hastings (1732-1818), first Governor-General of India.

WARWICK—**m** Place-name/surname derivation.

WAT—**m** Popular short form of Walter in medieval times. Wat Tyler (died 1381), leader of the Peasants' Revolt in 1381.

WAYNE—**m** 'Meadow' (Old English). Surname origin. Popularised by film star John Wayne (1907-79).

WENDELINE—**f** Diminutive of Wanda.

WENDY—**f** First written as a separate name by J. M. Barrie in *Peter Pan* (1904), inspired by a friend's little daughter who called him her 'friendy-wendy'. Also short for Gwendolen.

WESLEY—**m** Derived from the surname of the famous evangelist John Wesley (1703-91).

WESTON—**m** Place-name/surname derivation.

WILBUR—**m** 'Fortress of desire' (Old English). Wilbur Wright and brother Orville made the first powered aeroplane flight in 1903.

WILFRED, WILFRID—**m** 'Will for peace' (Old English). St Wilfrid (634-709), Bishop of York.

WILHELMINA—**f** Form of William. Queen of the Netherlands from 1890 to 1948.

WILLA—**f** Variant of Wilhelmina.

WILLARD—**m** 'Strong-willed' (Old English). Used mostly in USA.

WILLIAM—**m** 'Helmet of desire' (Teutonic). One of the most common male names since William the Conqueror. A line of kings of England to William IV (died 1837).

WILLIS—**m** 'Son of William' (Middle English).

WILLOUGHBY—**m** Place-name/surname derivation, used mostly to indicate mother's maiden name.

WILLOW—**f** Tree name in the tradition of Holly, Hazel etc.

WILMA—**f** Short form of Wilhelmina now used independently, especially in USA.

WILMER—**m** The masculine form of Wilma.

WILMOT—**m** Pet-name for William.

WINIFRED—**f** 'Friend of peace' (Old English). Also from Welsh Gwenfrewi, 'white wave'. St Winifred said to have been a Welsh princess martyred by Caradoc.

WINONA—**f** 'First-born' (Santee).

WINSTON—**m** From a surname, in turn from a place near Cirencester. There has been a Winston in the Churchill family since 1620.

WYSTAN—**m** Probably 'sacred stone' (Old English). St Wistan was a ninth-century prince of Mercia, murdered by his nephew Bertolf. Rarely used today but remembered as the name of the poet Wystan Hugh Auden (1907-73).

XANTHE—**f** 'Yellow' (Greek).

XAVIER—**m** St Francis Xavier (1506-52), one of the founders of the Society of Jesus or Jesuits.

XENA, XENIA—**f** 'Guest' or 'foreigner' (Greek).

XIMENA—**f** In Spanish legend, the wife of El Cid, the great ballad hero.

YASHWINA—**f** 'Successful' (Hindu).

YEHUDI—**m** 'Jew' (Hebrew). Greatest influence in its use is Sir Yehudi Menuhin (born 1916), virtuoso violinist.

YOLANDE—**f** An early variant of Viola.

YUL—**m** 'Beyond the horizon' (Mongolian). Made known in recent times through Yul Brynner, the film actor.

YURI—**m** 'Lily' (Hindu).

YVES—**m** French form of Ivo. Yves Montand, French actor and singer (1921-91).

YVETTE—**f** French diminutive of Yves.

YVONNE—**f** French diminutive form of Ivo.

ZACHARIAH, ZECHARIAH—**m** 'God's remembrance' (Hebrew). One of the prophetic books of the Old Testament.

ZADOC—**m** 'Just' (Hebrew).

ZAHRAH—**f** 'Beauty, star, flower' (Muslim).

ZARA, ZAHRA—**f** 'White' (Arabic). Zara Phillips (born 1981), the Princess Royal's second child.

ZED—**m** Short form of Zedekiah, used independently in the USA.

ZEDEKIAH—**m** 'The Lord is righteous' (Hebrew). The last king of Judah and Jerusalem (597-586 BC).

ZELDA—**f** Possibly introduced as a short form of Griselda, then used independently.

ZENA—**f** Variant of XENA

ZENOBIA—**f** 'Living through Zeus' (Greek). Third-century queen of Palmyra who dared to oppose Rome and was defeated by Aurelian in 272.

ZILLAH—**f** 'Shade' (Hebrew). Once a popular gypsy name.

ZIPPORAH—**f** 'Bird' (Hebrew). The wife of Moses (Exodus 2:21). Used regularly right down to the end of the nineteenth century.

ZOE—**f** 'Life' (Greek). A rendering of the Hebrew for Eve that is comparatively recent in Britain. Zoë, a Byzantine empress (980-1050), murdered her husband so that she could marry her lover.

ZOLA—**f** Fanciful invention based on Zoe.

ZUBAIDA—**f** 'Purity' (Muslim). Wife of Haroun Al-Raschid (786-809), Caliph of Baghdad.

ZULEIKA—**f** 'Brilliant beauty' (Persian). Favourite of Persian poets. *Zuleika Dobson* (1911) was a satirical novel by Max Beerbohm.

Further reading

Barnhart, C. L. (editor). *The New Century Cyclopaedia of Names* (three volumes). Appleton-Century-Crofts, 1954.

Coghlan, R. *Irish Christian Names*. Cassell, 1979.

Cresswell, Julia. *Bloomsbury Dictionary of First Names*. Bloomsbury, 1990.

Dunkling, L., and Gosling, W. *Everyman's Dictionary of First Names*. Dent, 1991.

Ferguson, Rosalind. *Choose Your Baby's Name*. Penguin, 1987.

First Names, a Pocket Guide. Collins, 1979.

Johnson, C. B., and Sleigh, L. *The Harrap Book of Boys' and Girls' Names*. Harrap, 1973.

Lockhart Ellefson, C. *The Melting Pot Book of Baby Names*. Betterway Publications, 1987.

Long, H. A. *Personal and Family Names*. Hamilton, Adams & Co., 1883.

Kitchin, M. *Choosing a Name, An A to Z of First Names and Their Meanings*. Hamlyn, 1979.

Malik, Z. A. *Muslim Names and Their Meanings*. Z Best Publications, 1983.

Merry, Emma. *First Names. The Definitive Guide to Popular Names in England and Wales, 1944-1994, and in the Regions, 1994*. HMSO, 1995.

Norman, Teresa. *A World of Baby Names*. Berkley, New York, 1996.

Rule, L. *Name Your Baby*. Bantam, 1986.

Shanta, Shrimati. *Handbook of Hindu Names*. Arnica International, Calcutta, 1969.

Spence, Hilary. *The Modern Book of Babies' Names*. Foulsham, 1975.

Stephens, R. *Welsh Names for Children*. Y Lolfa, 1975.

Swan, Helena. *Girls' Christian Names, Their History, Meaning and Association*. Tuttle, 1973.

Withycombe, E. G. *The Oxford Dictionary of English Christian Names*. Oxford University Press, third edition 1977.

Yonge, Charlotte M. *History of Christian Names*. 1884.